MW00331067

Emotional Intelligence

Emotional Intelligence

A *simple* and *actionable* guide to increasing performance, engagement and ownership

Amy Jacobson

WILEY

First published in 2021 by John Wiley & Sons Australia, Ltd
42 McDougall St, Milton Qld 4064
Office also in Melbourne

Typeset in FreightText Pro 10pt/13pt

© John Wiley & Sons Australia, Ltd 2021

The moral rights of the author have been asserted

ISBN: 978-0-730-39149-4

A catalogue record for this book is available from the National Library of Australia

All rights reserved. Except as permitted under the *Australian Copyright Act 1968* (for example, a fair dealing for the purposes of study, research, criticism or review), no part of this book may be reproduced, stored in a retrieval system, communicated or transmitted in any form or by any means without prior written permission. All inquiries should be made to the publisher at the address above.

Cover design by Wiley

Figure 2 'brain' image: © Sergey7777/Getty Images

Disclaimer
The material in this publication is of the nature of general comment only, and does not represent professional advice. It is not intended to provide specific guidance for particular circumstances and it should not be relied on as the basis for any decision to take action or not take action on any matter which it covers. Readers should obtain professional advice where appropriate, before making any such decision. To the maximum extent permitted by law, the author and publisher disclaim all responsibility and liability to any person, arising directly or indirectly from any person taking or not taking action based on the information in this publication.

Contents

Foreword

From Professor Gary Martin

Emotional intelligence, or lack of it, has become one of the most talked-about issues in our workplaces over the past decade.

With interest increasing over time, we now recognise that while our pure intellectual horsepower might help us to land a job, it's our emotional intelligence that determines exactly where we will end up in our careers.

In the broadest terms, our emotional intelligence is simply our capacity to deal effectively with our own emotions, and those of others.

In the workplace, our emotional intelligence supply is critical to our success as leaders and managers, or our effectiveness as members of a team.

In fact, emotional intelligence determines how confident we are, how we handle day-to-day interactions with others, and how we respond to conflict.

Despite being popularised by psychologist Daniel Goleman in the 1990s, decades later the concept of emotional intelligence has remained elusive to many.

It's still true that far too often those lacking even a modicum of emotional intelligence are completely in the dark over something that will almost certainly hold them back in both their working and personal lives.

Often misrepresented as a measure of someone's agreeableness, happiness, calmness or even optimism, confusion abounds when it comes to this powerful but seemingly inaccessible collective of important attributes.

That's where Amy Jacobson's *Emotional Intelligence: A simple and actionable guide to increasing performance, engagement and ownership* comes to the rescue.

This book takes the mystery out of the term through systematically unpacking the various layers of the concept's complexity and by providing practical ways to release our very own reservoir of emotional intelligence.

At the same time, *Emotional Intelligence* blasts away those unfortunate myths and misconceptions that have at times prevented all of us from sipping on what many workplace experts describe as an elixir of career success.

A warning though. This book will cause you to challenge your everyday behaviours even if you already consider yourself to be an emotionally intelligent person. By drawing you into a discussion on email communication, for example, you'll rapidly discover that much of your current e-communication is in urgent need of an emotional intelligence makeover.

Emotional Intelligence belongs on everyone's bookshelf. You'll want to read it and come back to it for actionable advice every time that you encounter a situation in which you did not put your most emotionally intelligent foot forward.

Taking the time to read this book is bound to set you on an emotional intelligence rollercoaster learning curve—one that will serve you well if you value the time you spend with family, friends and your work colleagues.

Professor Gary Martin FAIM FACE, Chief Executive Officer, The Australian Institute of Management in Western Australia

* * *

From G A (Geoff) Stewart

I have come to understand how important emotional intelligence is for any individual, especially how it can help them become better people, better team members, better leaders and a better organisation.

When I met Amy, I quickly realised how adept she is in the field of EI: it's why I use her to facilitate sessions with my teams. Her ability to communicate this topic in front of people has definitely transcended into a book that will no doubt become a reference tool for those looking to make change.

The subtitle 'a simple and actionable guide' is precisely what it is and the way she has laid it out through the use of plain speak and storytelling to reinforce her easy-to-follow steps ensures it is not daunting at all. In fact, while she lays out a challenge to you in doing something about your desire to grow, develop and constantly improve, you will feel she is there with you each step of the way. If you have been waiting for a reason to start, this is it.

G A (Geoff) Stewart APM, District Superintendent
South West District, Western Australia Police Force

About the author

Amy challenges and disrupts people's mindsets to own their performance and amplify engagement.

She is an emotional intelligence and human behaviour specialist with more than 19 years' experience in more than doubling engagement and market brand scores.

With her fascination with the human mind, neuroscience and neurolinguistic programming (NLP), Amy balances tough love and infectious energy to create purpose-driven teams that get results!

Amy takes people out of their comfort zone with her approach, challenging their mindset and helping them bring ownership and purpose to every work day.

Amy is driven to break through the misconception of EI to see people reach their full potential, embrace their strengths and find their ultimate purpose.

Based in Perth, Australia, with an international reach, Amy is a media personality across television, radio and print. She delivers keynotes, EI programs, workshops and coaching across all industries, sectors and individuals.

As a wife to her supporting husband and best friend Mark, mother to two amazing children, Amelia and Koen, business owner of Finding Your 'y' and co-founder and director of RISING QUEENS, Amy completely gets the challenge of balancing all of the roles in your life while still finding time to include yourself towards the top of the list.

Amy defines success as being happy. 'Find the things that make you happy and spend as much time as you can doing them. It really is that simple.' Travelling and adventures with her beautiful family is Amy's happiness, along with seeing people's faces light up as they find themselves.

For more information on Amy, to subscribe to her monthly educational newsletter, or to find out more about her services and clients, please visit: www.findingyoury.com.au.

Acknowledgements

This acknowledgement was harder to write than the book! I remember being told a story by one of my very first managers. His mum told him to never specifically name people in thank yous as there will always be someone you miss. This has stuck with me because the few times I have individually named people, I have missed someone. Hence my fear of writing an acknowledgement.

Let's start by thanking things that aren't human ... The road trip to Monkey Mia that allowed me huge blocks of time to evacuate the things in my mind into this book. Old Gold almond chocolate, which was my obsession and kept me on my sugar high. The lounge cushion that sat on my lap under my laptop as I typed on a Friday night. The words never seem to come during the day or at my desk. The cushion is a blocker as much as a comfort, with me wondering whether a laptop on my lap will lead to cancer of the crotch. Okay, enough of that, let's get to the humans that I adore!

To my forever supportive husband, Mark, who has listened and watched me change my path and become ridiculously excited and caught up in the moment so many times in this confusing world, and who still believes that I can do anything I put my mind to: I love you dearly.

My gorgeous children, Amelia and Koen, who have always seen me through rose-coloured glasses, embraced my crazy, and my (at times) embarrassing need to be the 'fun' and 'cool' mum. I'm so thankful that you chose me to be your mum. I will continue to love you every minute of every day. You are my world!

My amazing family and dearest friends: this book wouldn't have happened without all of you. In fact, I wouldn't be where I am today without you all. Thank you from the bottom of my heart, I love you all. Some of the hilarious examples or suggestions you gave me to try to get your name into this book were unfortunately not quite appropriate, especially for an EI book. But hey, there is always a chance for a second book!

To my advisors, support network and all of the people I have crossed paths in my life: thank you for the teachings and the learnings. There is always something to learn, whether we are learning what *not* to do or what it takes to be an amazing person, leader and best version of ourselves.

Thank you xx

Introduction

I was sitting next to a gentleman at a seminar in early 2019 when we were asked to turn to the person next to us and talk about some of the biggest blockages in the workplace.

I had taken my seat just as the seminar commenced and was yet to meet him. He turned out to be a very friendly, highly respected author and an experienced leadership and performance consultant with more than 30 years' experience. He turned to me and said, 'On a side note from the biggest blockages, you know what drives me crazy? These new, so-called emotional intelligence specialists that are coming into businesses and softening everyone up. You know, where no-one can do wrong, everyone is hard done by and everyone is always right.'

At this point, he knew my name but had no idea what I did for a living. For the next few minutes, I listened to him tell me exactly what he thought of these 'so-called emotional intelligence specialists' before the activity ended and our attention refocused on the seminar speaker. At the end of the seminar, he instantly turned to me to continue to vent his very emotional frustrations but instead I asked him to tell me more about what he did.

His face instantly lit up as he started to speak of his true passion. I heard all about the amazing new book he was finalising, which had been inspired by well-known leadership figures, including big names such as Simon Sinek. The book encompasses areas such as building performance, communication and other leadership skills. I could hear his love for what he did, and I told him that I couldn't wait to read his book as it definitely aligned to my passion as well. It was at that point that he asked me, 'So Amy, what do you do?' I answered, 'I specialise in emotional intelligence.'

Yes, an awkward silence followed before he apologised if he had offended me, but commented that he still stood strongly by everything he said. Of course I wasn't offended; it didn't offend or shock me.

Emotional intelligence is a broad term that is misunderstood by many. There are so many misconceptions relating to the meaning of emotional intelligence and what it comprises.

Some people picture emotional intelligence as a soft skill that wraps cotton wool around people, making them feel good, with positive affirmations. Maybe throw in a few lollipops, rainbows and an 'everyone's a winner' approach and we are set!

Others think that it is all about getting in touch with our feelings—being highly emotional—or only for psychologists.

This is what continues to drive me. It drives me to break through the misconceptions. To create a social impact by educating others about the benefits of emotional intelligence in the workplace and in life. To help others to understand and build their emotional intelligence in order to truly own their performance and amplify engagement.

Why emotional intelligence?

Every single thing in this world has been created to satisfy a human emotional need. Every product, every industry, every service. The purpose is to create the desired emotional outcome based on the reason why the product/industry/service was created in the first place.

Whenever there are humans involved, the level of emotional intelligence (or EI) is the key contributor to an outcome's success. Within the workplace, we bring people of different skills, personalities, backgrounds, beliefs and values together.

Emotional intelligence is not about what we know or what we can do; it's all about how and why we do what we do. It's about understanding what makes each and every one of us 'tick', why we react the way we do and how to control and leverage the way we react to achieve the very best outcome for everyone.

> ## Emotional intelligence is every single human behaviour and emotional reaction that drives the events, and the outcomes, of what is happening around us.

In high-pressure environments, where we deal directly with people and their emotions, our degree of emotional intelligence can either resolve or exacerbate a situation. Research by the Carnegie Institute of Technology shows that up to 85 per cent of our success is due to skills in 'human engineering' rather than technical skills.

As we encounter different situations, different people with different communication styles and an everchanging workplace, it is our EI that determines our success in achieving desired outcomes.

Technical skills may get us the job or start the business, but it's our EI skills that get us promotions and a successful business.

How are your current emotional intelligence levels contributing to your success and the overall success of the people around you?

Is it EQ or EI?

Emotional intelligence can be referred to as both EQ and EI. So what is the difference?

EI is the abbreviation for emotional intelligence and refers to the core concepts and meaning of emotional intelligence.

EQ is the abbreviation for emotional quotient, which is the score achieved after measuring our level of emotional intelligence based on certain core concepts. EQ aligns to the use of the abbreviation IQ (intelligence quotient) and other quotient measures. IQ is never referred to as HI (human intelligence) or anything other than IQ, whether we are referencing the quotient score or the core concepts.

For this reason, it has become commonplace to refer to emotional intelligence in the same manner and call it EQ. Both terms are relevant and understood as being emotional intelligence.

For the purpose of this book, we will refer to emotional intelligence using the abbreviation EI.

Is EI more important than IQ?

There is an ongoing debate as to whether EI is more important than IQ, with opinions differing depending on who we talk to. It's like the 'which came first, the chicken or the egg?' debate.

EI and IQ are part of who we are. Every human has both EI and IQ; however, the amount of each differs from one person to another. Each circumstance requires a degree of EI and IQ in order to identify, assess, develop and resolve a situation.

IQ is required in learning environments; EI is always required in order to communicate or deliver IQ. It takes flexibility and adaptability to the situation, and the people involved, to get the right balance between EI and IQ.

Overall, neither is more important than the other. EI will only get us so far without a certain level of IQ. Likewise, IQ will only get us so far without a certain level of EI skills. Balance and adaptability are what really matter.

About the book

This book is divided into three parts. Part I examines emotional intelligence and its history, whether EI is innate or learnt and how it is measured.

In part II, I introduce you to my five-step process for disrupting your mindset to increase performance and amplify engagement. I call it The EI Rewiring Process.

Part III explores the importance of EI in the future, focusing in particular on the workplace and the significance of EI in an AI world.

Part I

What is emotional intelligence?

While the popularity of the concept of emotional intelligence continues to increase, it is certainly not a new concept. It still has many questioning whether it really can be taught or whether we are born with it.

How do we measure how emotionally intelligent we are?

Chapter 1

The history of emotional intelligence

The term 'emotional intelligence' was coined by psychologists Peter Salovey and John Mayer in their 1990 article published in the journal *Imagination, Cognition and Personality* titled 'Emotional intelligence'.

Their definition reads:

> Emotional intelligence is the ability to perceive emotions, to access and generate emotions so as to assist thought, to understand emotions and emotional knowledge, and to reflectively regulate emotions so as to promote emotional and intellectual growth.

This was the first time the words 'emotional intelligence' appeared in a publication. However, references to how we get along with the people around us existed as concepts as early as 1920 through the work of Edward Thorndike, although at that time they were labelled 'social intelligence'. Emotional intelligence was yet to be referenced.

It wasn't until 1995, when Daniel Goleman published his book *Emotional Intelligence: Why it can matter more than IQ*, that the concept of EI really became a popular and more well-known term.

In his book, Goleman talks about the five components of EI as:

1. self-awareness

2. self-regulation

3. internal motivation

4. empathy

5. social skills.

Today, this remains one of the most common explanations of EI, but for many people, it can be confusing.

For example, what do self-awareness and self-regulation consist of? What's the difference between empathy and sympathy? We require a certain level of emotional intelligence to understand what these components actually mean!

Before we analyse EI in depth in part II using my five-step, action-based mindset disruption process, let's answer a couple of the most frequently asked questions.

Chapter 2

Can EI be taught or are we born with it?

Some people are definitely born with EI. This kind of research is extremely hard to prove, but we see some children naturally display levels of EI at a very young age—whether it is empathising with other children and adults, knowing what they like and dislike without overthinking and fear of judgement, or asking 'why' to understand the purpose.

I remember the first time my daughter Amelia really cried during a movie. She was four years old and we were watching the movie *Red Dog*. There is quite an emotional scene towards the end of the movie. (I won't describe it in case you haven't seen it.) She had tears running down her face and was so confused. The emotional response wasn't spelled out to her like children's movies tend to do—this was a family movie telling a story and leaving the emotional reaction completely up to the viewer. Amelia's emotions latched on and the tears were heartfelt, triggering her EI to *feel* what others were feeling.

We see children comforting other children or adults and knowing exactly what to say in the moment to help them feel better—a great display of empathy. They know what they like, they know what makes them happy and they are motivated to make it happen.

There are many adults who have a high level of EI yet may not recognise it as EI. To them, it's just who they are and have always been. Since they don't recognise this as their EI, they may struggle to help others develop skills and behaviours like their own. Again, it's like it's in their DNA—a no-brainer, they might say—it just happens naturally.

Then there are others who lack EI in certain areas and are very aware of this. They are proactively looking for ways to learn and further develop their EI knowing that they can be better in themselves and that the impact they have on those around them can also improve.

EI can be taught. I've taught many people in this field. The key is, you must want to learn it.

We must commit to continually recognising the need, reframing and reviewing. Reading a book on EI, or attending a seminar, won't make us emotionally intelligent. It's an ongoing process and something that we have to work at daily. We learn the concepts and tools in order to consistently implement them.

One of my best friends once said: 'A marriage is something you work on every day to help it grow and be great.' EI is very much the same: it takes awareness, work and ongoing development because every situation and person is different.

Lastly, there are people who are in desperate need of developing their EI but are simply not aware of this—nor do they have an interest in doing so. Unless we can reach the first stage of self-awareness and *own* the need to improve, unfortunately our growth will be limited. We must want to grow and develop our EI in order to truly learn it.

I often wonder whether we were all born with high levels of EI and as we age and experience life and with it many defining moments, whether our level of EI decreases or stays the same. We know that defining moments throughout our lives directly impact our beliefs and values, controlling our mindset, self-worth and confidence levels.

They also determine what makes us tick: our emotional response, the way we treat others, how we communicate and our levels of motivation. It only takes one unexpected situation or defining moment to have us questioning how we will approach a situation should it arise again. So maybe our EI levels are high when we are born and some people are able to maintain those high levels, while those of others decrease or get pushed further into their subconscious mind as those defining moments—and 'life'—happen.

Extensive research has been done for the Association for Psychological Science at a deeper level asking whether we are born with our purpose built into our DNA or whether we develop it through life. What's interesting is the thought that if it's in our DNA, research notes that we are more convinced that it will bring us endless motivation, happiness and success.

This then restricts how open we are to other developments or challenges because we are committed to our built-in purpose. If things don't work out exactly how we expected, then it must not have been our purpose so we give up.

In contrast, those who believe we develop purpose are more open to learning, adding new skills and facing challenges without giving up because they know how hard they have worked and how badly they want it.

I believe it's more of a hybrid model. We are born with natural talent and skills in certain areas, but we also have the ability to learn in every area. It comes down to how badly we want it and what we are willing to do.

If we can bring the balance of our purpose together with high EI skills, we are certainly in a great position for success.

Chapter 3

How do we measure EI?

Measuring any type of human behaviour, reaction, personality, characteristic or emotion is always a challenge. Although all human minds have the same structure and functionality, the content, triggers and usage are completely different. Each and every one of us is completely unique so the process can never be 100 per cent accurate.

There are many free EI assessments that can be found simply by searching the internet. There are also personality tests and quizzes that complement the EI assessments to paint a more inclusive picture of our personality.

All these assessments involve a number of questions that the applicant answers, resulting in them being placed into a defined category that measures their EI or personality. The assessments are fun and seem scarily accurate at times. The categories are the creator's definition of EI or types of personality.

However, this can result in the person sitting the assessment lacking ownership of their results. We might find ourselves justifying why we are different and therefore why a result doesn't apply to us: 'I can't increase my score in empathy because that's just not who I am.' Or we get our scores and accept that is who we are rather than ascertaining how to grow and become what we are truly capable of.

I much prefer to reverse the process of defining how an emotionally intelligent person behaves and having us assess ourselves based on our own definitions, capability and realistic delivery.

So, what are the characteristics of an emotionally intelligent person?

I use the following eight statements to define emotionally intelligent people:

1. They listen and learn from criticism.

2. They maintain a positive (solution mode) attitude in difficult situations.

3. They manage anxiety, fear, anger and all emotions appropriately in all situations.

4. They recognise how their behaviour affects others.

5. They are empathetic.

6. They have discipline and are self-motivated.

7. They listen even if they disagree.

8. They look for ways to improve when things don't go to plan.

The assessment approach I use is to ask the person to read the statements above and think about how they would feel if they were in a situation where one of the eight statements might apply.

Let's use the first statement as an example.

I ask you to do a report for me. You deliver it on time and I'm now sitting in front of you saying that it isn't what I wanted. You have not delivered what I was expecting—it does not contain the level of detail that I require. I'm going to need you to do it again. How are you feeling hearing this in relation to the first statement, 'Listen and learn from criticism'?

Score yourself out of 10 based on 10 being, *100 per cent comfortable with the feedback—ready to go and give it another shot*; and 1 being, *I'm absolutely staggered to hear that—it makes me feel angry, upset and annoyed | it makes me feel a level of frustration.*

As soon as we picture a number on this scale in our mind, we have automatically defined what a 1 and what a 10 look like. Your definition of a 10 will look very different from my 10 and anyone else's 10. What we do know is that the 10 that you just defined in your mind is 100 per cent realistic and achievable by you!

Our mind cannot create a 10 that is not a realistic or achievable version of us. It is your definition and you know you are capable of it. It's not my definition. It's not a quiz or assessment that has been predefined—you own that definition and that 10 out of 10.

If your own score was not a 10 out of 10, what is stopping you from becoming a 10 out of 10? What are your blockers?

We have identified what we are really capable of and we also know what our current state is. There must be something that is stopping us from being our ideal 10 out of 10 right now. What is it?

We now have the opportunity to look for ways to develop and bridge that gap. As humans, when we are given a 'current state' and 'future state' or a scale from 1 to 10, we naturally want the ultimate prize ... the 10! Trying to jump straight from our current state to the ultimate prize is when things can become overwhelming or all too hard and we tend to give up when it doesn't happen overnight. I see this with many people when setting goals.

The key here is to think about what it would take to increase your score by just 1 point. So, if we are currently a 6 out of 10, how do we become a 7 out of 10? What is one simple thing that we could do that would mean our own rating would become a 7 rather than a 6? Taking it one step at a time.

You can use table 1 as a tool to go through each of the eight statements, score yourself out of 10, identify any blockers that are stopping you from getting a 10/10 and think about development opportunities that would enable you to increase your score.

Table 1: score yourself

Characteristic	Self-rating	Blockers	Development
1 Listen and learn from criticism			
2 Maintain a solution mode attitude			
3 Manage emotions			
4 Recognise behavioural effect on others			
5 Empathise			
6 Be disciplined and self-motivated			
7 Listen			
8 Look for ways to improve			

Measuring our EI empowers us with total ownership. It's our definition, our score, our blockers, our ways to increase our EI. There is no-one else to blame and no justification as to why it can't happen. In other words, we *own* it!

* * *

Okay, now it's time to take emotional intelligence, simplify it and turn it into relatable and actionable concepts using a five-step process that I call The EI Rewiring Process.

Part II

Disrupting mindsets using EI

Even with the evolution of the definition of emotional intelligence, the concept remains confusing to many. As I pointed out in chapter 1, there needs to be a level of EI education to understand what Goleman's five components of EI even mean. For many, the core concepts themselves are not everyday words, nor are they easy to remember.

I'm a big fan of simplicity and action. The human brain always responds well to a 'call-to-action', especially when we can relate to simple and familiar words. For this reason, I created The EI Rewiring Process, a simple, five-step, action-based process incorporating and expanding on Goleman's five components of EI to disrupt mindsets in order to own performance and amplify engagement. The five stages are:

1. *Own it*: Becoming self-aware and owning who we are

2. *Face it*: Controlling our emotions and working with them

3. *Feel it*: Understanding others and the impact we have on them

4. *Ask it*: Communicating with influence and purpose

5. *Drive it*: Being motivated and reaching our full potential.

Let's explore these stages together to understand what they mean and the benefits that accompany them.

Chapter 4

The EI Rewiring Process

In order to really disrupt our mindset, we must understand the process our mind goes through.

Similarly to grief and change, our mindset and emotional reactions go through a process that aligns to The EI Rewiring Process. We generally have a default emotional response when something unexpected occurs, with some of us instantly feeling fear, anger, confusion or even excitement. It's not until we can *own* the situation and our reaction that we can move on to *face* the reality of the situation, make decisions and mitigate where required.

Owning and facing are the self-awareness and self-regulation stages. Conquering these means we can step out of our own mind and start to *feel* the impact on those around us. This is where empathy, leadership and true people skills are brought to the forefront. Understanding and being able to read what others are going through or what makes them 'tick' gives us the ability to *ask* the right questions.

Communication, still to this day, is the make or break of many conversations, relationships and organisations. It is also the way we *ask* and *feel* that leads to the *drive*: the ability to motivate and inspire not only those around us, but, more importantly, ourselves to get results.

While all of us go through this process, the speed at which it happens differs. Some of us can fly through the process and be ready to *drive* out the other end within days, or even hours. Others may get stuck in one of the early stages for years and even be triggered to return back to previous stages along the way.

During the COVID-19 pandemic, we noticed the vast difference in how people were coping and what stage of the process they were at. As humans, we assume that the stage we are at is where other people are at too. We therefore tend to approach situations based on our current mindset.

I was part of a virtual program during the early stages of the pandemic and we were having this very discussion. One of the ladies in the program was in her mid-sixties and she spoke up with great commitment, saying, 'Amy, I know exactly what you mean! My children are calling me every single morning to check in and see if I'm okay and if there is anything that I need. I know they mean well by it, and I'm really thankful, but *I am fine!* I wish they would just leave me alone.'

This is a perfect example of where her children were very much at the *feel it* and *ask it* stage, yet she was well and truly at the *drive it* stage. She had gone through the process and was ready to move full steam ahead. Trying to pull her back to the earlier stages was frustrating her.

Similarly, I worked with a lot of organisations in those early COVID-19 days to ensure their staff had the right level of support to get through the circumstances.

I came across a comparable situation in that I saw numerous team members who had moved through The EI Rewiring Process into *drive it* only for their leader to drown them with too much care because he was still in the *feel it* stage. This frustrated most of them but also made them start to question whether they had underreacted, and that maybe they should be more concerned and should be struggling more than they were: *What were they missing? What did others know that they didn't?* I saw several of these people being dragged back to the very beginning of the process with the 'fear factor' returning simply because he was still in the *feel it* stage thinking he was doing the right thing.

This isn't only prevalent during pandemics; this occurs every day in the workplace when unexpected or unplanned situations or decisions occur. It can even happen during a conversation, with our mind racing through the process within seconds, or in some situations getting stuck in those earlier stages and creating an absolute blockage to the conversation.

EI is not about learning what to do in every single situation. It is about understanding the process; recognising the core concepts and attributes; and knowing how to apply, adapt and deliver at each step of the process based on the needs of the person in front of you. This is how we truly disrupt mindsets.

It is about rewiring our brains with emotional intelligence to directly impact performance, outcomes and engagement levels.

Okay, so let's now begin to unpack The EI Rewiring Process.

Chapter 5

Own it: Becoming self-aware and owning who we are

'Owning it' is an easy way to summarise emotional intelligence in one short statement. It relates to owning our mindset, owning our situation, owning the impact we have on those around us, owning our communication ability, and owning our performance and motivation. It's about owning our life knowing that no-one else is responsible, or to blame, for what we have or haven't done.

It's where we start, yet it flows through every part of EI. Let's begin by understanding how the mind works.

The emotional mind

Sigmund Freud's model of the awareness of the human mind details three levels:

1. the unconscious mind

2. the conscious mind

3. the subconscious mind.

Let's break down what each of the levels means in simple terms.

The unconscious mind is basically what keeps us alive, with its usage estimated at 30 to 40 per cent of our mind's capacity. It ensures our organs are all functioning and our body is doing what it needs to do to survive. Nice and simple.

The conscious mind is the front end of our mind, and its usage is estimated at 10 per cent. It's responsible for quick responses. You know those moments when we say something and then think, 'Why did I say that?' or 'I probably shouldn't have said that!' We can thank our conscious mind for that quick, sometimes inappropriate, response. It also analyses all incoming data, so, for example, everything we read in a book will enter through our conscious mind before either going into our subconscious mind or being forgotten.

Our conscious mind holds many factual and simple answers along with the ability to focus, while at the same time our subconscious mind can be thinking of something completely different.

Have you ever been driving somewhere and your mind is thinking about what you will cook for dinner that night or the report that you need to complete, and all of a sudden you magically arrive at your destination thinking, 'How did I get here? Was I doing the speed limit?'

This is our talented conscious mind's ability to focus.

Now don't confuse this with multitasking. This is the conscious mind on autopilot, rather than needing to actively think or learn something, and we know that neither of the things that our conscious or subconscious mind are concentrating on is getting our full attention. Research says that our mind does not have the ability to multitask: it jumps back and forth between tasks, so we are not truly 'multitasking'. It's more like we're doing several things alongside one another.

Picture yourself in the kitchen cooking a new recipe while having your current TV series obsession playing in front of you. When you are cooking a brand-new recipe, it requires focus and brain power to create this new memory. Our mind is not working off an existing memory. Our ability to follow this recipe and actually take in the TV episode at the same time becomes extremely challenging and it's unlikely to be able to be done. The recipe also takes quite a while to cook.

Let's swap that now for a dinner that you have cooked numerous times that you don't require the recipe for and know how to make. Your ability to do this while watching your TV episode becomes a lot easier and you will take more of the episode in. You are still not completely focused on either of them; however, the cooking is tapping into your long-term memory and running on 'autopilot' while your conscious mind is taking in the TV episode. The cooking requires very little of your mind power.

The more competent we are at the task at hand, and the less new learning our brain is doing, the less our mind needs to switch back and forth between tasks.

> What I love the most about the conscious mind is that it presents factual information to the subconscious mind asking for the correct emotional response.

Living within our subconscious mind are our emotions, values, beliefs, habits and long-term memory. Our subconscious mind's usage is estimated at 50 to 60 per cent, with many researchers suggesting that it is 30 000 times more powerful than the conscious mind! That's huge, right? When we know how to utilise and leverage our subconscious mind, we ultimately influence the outcome and our level of success.

So, our conscious mind turns to our subconscious mind and delivers the situation: 'It's Monday morning, the middle of winter, raining outside, it's a workday … how do I feel about this?'

Our subconscious mind taps into our beliefs, our values, our long-term memory and finds out how we feel about Mondays, winter, rain and work. It works together with our amygdala (the part of our brain that is responsible for our emotions) to generate our emotional response to the situation. This response is then delivered through every part of our body and drives our mindset.

The need to be right!

If our emotional response is not in favour of a situation, we may find our body slouching, our energy lacking and we may start to look for reasons to justify our mindset. As humans, we have been programmed since we were kids to be right. All through our childhood and in particular during our schooling years, we have been rewarded for being 'right' based on our grades and our behaviour.

It's no surprise that as adults, we also like to be right. So, when our mindset decides that 'I don't like this' and 'it's not going to be a good day', it starts looking for confirmation or validation to show it is correct. You know those moments when we start to say 'of course': *Of course I got every red light on the way to work. Of course I just missed the train by seconds. Of course my first customer is angry.* That is our subconscious mind validating our mindset to prove that we are right! If someone tries to tell us otherwise, they are wrong because if they were right, that would make us wrong and we don't like to be wrong!

On the reverse side, if our subconscious mind and amygdala tell us 'yes, we love Mondays / we love winter / rain is great / I like going to work', then our energy levels lift. We might even get a bit of a bounce in our step and our mindset is now looking for confirmation or validation to show it is a great day!

We know that every day brings with it the opportunity to be both optimistic and pessimistic. We can choose our mood and how we will react. This is basically the only real thing we have control of in this world—our emotions and how we choose to react.

> It's not the day, it's not the circumstances, it's not the people around us that make us feel the way we do. Ultimately, it's 100 per cent us and our mindset.

When our conscious mind delivers the facts to our subconscious mind—which holds our values, beliefs and long-term memories—we decide how we feel and what our mindset will be. It's our choice, and it's time to *own it*!

Tapping into the subconscious mind

Now that we understand the three levels of the mind, the challenge is knowing how to move through the conscious mind and tap into the subconscious mind as much as possible. In order to learn or build our EI, we need to be in our subconscious mind.

There are three ways to reach our subconscious mind:

- using the power of the pause
- challenging or confusing the conscious mind
- asking the same type of question 5 to 7 times.

The power of the pause

The power of the pause is having the ability to ask a question, then pause ... Even after the other person answers the question, we continue to pause ... As humans, we have been encouraged to talk from the moment we were born. So much so, that silences can become awkward. When faced with those awkward silences, we tend to talk to fill the silence and avoid the awkward feeling.

The first response is likely to come straight from the conscious mind and as the conscious mind gets confused by the silence or starts to feel awkward, it will turn to the subconscious mind for help. Our emotional mind starts to answer the silence by incorporating our values, beliefs, long-term memories and experiences. This is when we tend to hear how someone is really feeling. Even when we know someone is using the 'power of the pause' with us, it is very hard not to want to fill that silence.

This is a fantastic tool to use in a sales environment, leadership conversation, Q&A time at an event or in a meeting, and even as parents we tend to use it on our children. The longer we pause, the deeper the other person will go in their mind and the more raw and emotionally honest the answer tends to be. I will address this in more detail in chapter 8.

Challenging or confusing the conscious mind

The conscious mind handles and tends to triage any questions, requests or activities. The second way to tap into the subconscious mind is to really challenge or confuse the conscious mind. When it can't answer the question easily, it feels the need to engage the subconscious mind for assistance.

There is an 'ice breaker' activity that I use at the start of a workshop to get the audience into their subconscious mind ready to learn and grow their emotional intelligence. With no notice, I ask them to turn to the person beside them and to tell them their life story in one minute. Following this, again with no notice, I ask them to tell their story in a completely different way in one minute.

The results show that the first time the story is told, it is extremely factual. It comes straight from our conscious mind and tends to include our name, age, occupation, family set-up, where we live, and so on—that is, automatic responses that our conscious mind can handle.

It's not until the second time, when we are asked to tell our story in a different way, that our conscious mind gets confused and turns to our subconscious mind for help. At this stage, we start to respond on a more personal level, talking about the things we are passionate about or parts of our life in more detail. Our language tends to change to more descriptive words and the story gets a lot deeper. This comes from the values, beliefs and long-term memories in our subconscious mind.

I have had some extremely creative people tell their second story in a different language, through dance and even through their husband's and dog's eyes! Every one of these responses required the person to delve into their subconscious mind, which was ultimately the aim of the activity.

Asking the same type of question 5 to 7 times

There are many techniques used across industries in relation to training or problem solving incorporating '7 questions' or '5 whys' to reach the core problem or to access the best of ideas. The reason why these techniques work is because as each question is asked, we go deeper into our mind, through the conscious mind and into the subconscious mind.

Remembering that everything we do in life is for an emotional outcome, this emotional outcome is triggered and influenced by our emotional mind. When we continue to ask questions, we continue to remove the superficial thoughts or consequences being driven by the core problem. For most people, it is once we hit the fifth to seventh time of asking the same question that we tap into the subconscious mind and reveal the core.

I run an exercise in one of my workshops to manage our 'busy' that asks the attendees to list seven ways they are interrupted during their workday. The first two answers tend to be phone calls and emails. I've noticed that, on average, the first four answers are all ways that other people interrupt them. The items listed after that are the ways they interrupt themselves, such as getting hungry, being distracted, needing to go the toilet or scrolling through social media.

Similarly, I have a coaching exercise where I ask the client to identify a way to improve their current satisfaction levels. I then ask them, 'What's another way?', 'What about another one?', 'Give me one more' and again the results show that the first few ideas are simple and easy to implement. The last few ideas are the ones that really matter and are driving the emotional triggers and outcome. They are usually the most confronting or challenging to implement but they make the biggest difference.

As children, we go through the stage of asking, 'Why?' to everything. The answers often result in another 'why' question. As children continue to ask us 'Why?', it really gets us thinking and can confuse us or even frustrate us because it takes us into our subconscious mind and makes us question it as well. I wish that as adults we would ask the question 'Why?' more often. *Why are we sending this email, why are we feeling this way, why are we responding in that manner, why are we doing this, why do we choose to work where we do, why is paying this bill important ...* we create so much more clarity and purpose simply by asking the question 'Why?'

Some people will reach this point before the fifth to seventh question. These people are either already in an emotional state—so they are already tapping into their subconscious mind—or they may have high emotional intelligence and are able to move through to the subconscious mind faster.

Any time we make a list asking for a number of answers to the same question, we are best to flip the list upside down and start with the last answer. This is the one that has come from deep in the subconscious mind. This is the one that is powering our emotional driver. This is the one that is likely to be the toughest to deliver but it will also make the biggest difference!

What are our beliefs and values?

The responses from our emotional mind are heavily driven by our beliefs and values.

> Whether a situation aligns with or challenges
> our current beliefs and values will play an
> important role in our ability to respond
> in an emotionally intelligent way.

So, what are beliefs and values and where do they come from?

Our beliefs and values start to form from the minute we are born, which raises the question of whether they may be able to be passed through our DNA. For the purpose of this book, we are going to concentrate on the creation of our beliefs and values after we are born.

It is in the first seven years of our life that our core beliefs and values are formed. Our beliefs are opinions or things that we hold to be true and important.

Our values are what we put in place to protect our beliefs. For example, if I had a belief that to be the best version of me my health and fitness should always be a priority, then I might value gyms and personal trainers being readily available and accessible. Or if I had a belief that I was terrible at public speaking, I might value those people who love it and will volunteer, saving me from having to do it.

There doesn't need to be any proof, validation or reasoning behind our beliefs to prove them right or wrong. My beliefs will be different from your beliefs—every person holds their own version of beliefs.

These beliefs are formed based on our environment, family, friends, experiences and memories. After the age of seven, whenever a circumstance happens in life that is substantial enough to question our core beliefs and values, we create new beliefs and values or alter our existing ones. These are referred to as defining moments.

> I had a 46-year-old male client — let's call him Adam — who worked extremely long hours, was very driven and committed to his job and was constantly looking for success. It didn't matter what he achieved, it never quite seemed enough. The drive to succeed was impacting his family life and his ability to regulate his emotions. His belief was that in order to succeed he needed to be the very best at what he did, hold the most senior role in his department and meet his definition of 'wealthy'. We started to reflect to find out when this belief of success was created and what was driving it.
>
> When Adam was 13 and in Year 8 at school, he could recall being in Mrs Stewart's Maths class and being asked to answer a question in front of the class. Maths was not his strong point and not only was Adam's answer wrong, Mrs Stewart proceeded to ridicule him in front of the class, questioning how he could ever amount to anything if he couldn't even understand Year 8 Maths.
>
> This was a defining moment for Adam. For some, this defining moment may have created a belief of failure, but for Adam, it created a new belief that he *would* amount to something, be very successful and prove Mrs Stewart wrong. In creating this belief, 13-year-old Adam defined 'success' in his mind as a high-level job title and substantial wealth. Values were then created to protect and embed this belief: hard working, job success and wealth.
>
> At 46, this belief was still driving Adam, yet the measure of success that it was based on was materialistic items rather than the true emotional driver and outcome — that is, the emotional driver, in his case, of feeling 'worthy' and being 'happy'.

It takes some of us a long time to work out that the true measure of success, as corny as it can sound, is happiness. There are many people who are wealthy yet unhappy, while there are many others who have little wealth, yet are the most genuinely happy people I have ever met. Success, for me, is the feeling of happiness with who we are and what we have. It really is that simple.

What is it that makes you happy?

Beliefs and values can continue to change throughout our lives based on new defining moments. It is also possible to change our beliefs and values by identifying how they were created and reframing the situation in order to create new ones.

We see beliefs change in families as children grow through their religious beliefs, political alignment and even the sporting teams they follow. As children, we tend to align to our parents' beliefs. Many children don't get to choose which sporting team jersey they wear or which team they cheer on in those earlier years.

As an adult, I have developed a strong belief that 'good people' are not deceitful and don't lie, nor do they steal. For this reason, I highly value honesty and transparency as two of the greatest personality traits in people I am surrounded by. I am sure there are many beliefs that you hold to be true and have created values to protect these beliefs.

As time passes, we experience defining moments that create new beliefs, new values and new alignments to sporting teams, religions, politics—pretty much everything in life.

Our emotional response and mindset are guided by these values and beliefs, with our responses being dependent on whether a situation supports or questions our values and beliefs.

Be the chihuahua

We've already spoken about the power of our mindset being driven from our subconscious mind, but when we add in our beliefs and values, this power reaches another level. The age-old story of 'fight or flight' is always a great way to explain the real power of bringing them all together.

My favourite analogy is when we picture two dogs—a chihuahua and a German shepherd—walking along a street and coming face to face ... well, almost face-to-face! Given that chihuahuas are generally less than 25 cm tall and German shepherds stand at up to 66 cm in height, both heads will be tilted when they decide they don't like each other.

Now all physical characteristics of these two breeds of dog, from the height to the weight, jaw size and speed, tell us that the chihuahua is out of its league should this turn into a fight. But against all odds, that chihuahua looks up at the German shepherd and thinks, 'I've got this!' Nine times out of 10, the chihuahua will shape up ready to fight, and the German shepherd will look at the chihuahua completely confused, or even laughing to itself, thinking, 'What is this dog thinking?' There is a chance the German shepherd may even be scared of the chihuahua.

What I truly love about this story is that there is only one thing telling the chihuahua that it's 'got this' and that's its mindset. Nothing on paper, no physical features, no statistics support this, but the chihuahua's mindset overrides everything, absolutely owning the situation to the point that it makes the German shepherd question either itself or the situation.

Do you doubt yourself or are you a chihuahua?

This scenario happens every day in the workplace and in life in general. We judge ourselves on paper compared to others. 'How do I compare with qualifications, years of experience, job title, age, gender, looks?' ... and the list goes on. This paper or physical assessment sends our mindset into a spin deciding whether we belong in this room and at this table, whether we will speak up in the conversation, whether we have earned our spot, whether we have anything of value to add ...

> I was working with a 33-year-old female client, Jayde, who was in an executive role for a boutique medium-sized business. She was extremely good at what she did in an industry dominated by middle-aged males. Jayde had been invited to a high-level management conference interstate. She was very excited to be selected to attend what was going to be an educational and fantastic growth opportunity. She was, however, nervous about walking into the room for the first time and unsure whether she would feel she belonged with the other attendees.
>
> I shared the chihuahua and German shepherd story with her and challenged Jayde to 'be the chihuahua!' Her ability, achievements and value-add to the room was not in doubt. Her fear of judgement,

(continued)

paper characteristics and feeling of inclusivity with the audience was the concern. This related wholeheartedly to her mindset and that's what we worked on.

Jayde sent me a picture of a chihuahua after the first day of the conference. She had walked into that room channelling the confidence of a chihuahua knowing that she brought value to that room and knowing that she belonged there. Jayde walked away from the conference with so many learnings, made significant contributions and others learned from her. She also walked away with many new connections and a confidence in her step and ability.

Default modalities

While our values and beliefs are the core of our emotions and mindset, our modalities determine how fast and how well we take in information that will potentially align or create a trigger.

In NLP (neurolinguistic programming) terms, our modalities are the ways in which we learn, communicate and make decisions; for example, the process our mind goes through when we decide to make a purchase.

There are four main modalities: visual, auditory, kinaesthetic and digital. Research suggests that our modalities are the main driver for our ability to learn.

Every single one of us has and uses these modalities to learn and make decisions. However, we each have a default modality, which is the one modality that is more dominant than the other three. If the style in which information is communicated to us matches our dominant—or default—modality, our ability and speed to absorb and learn dramatically increases.

Do you know what your default modality is?

Visual

Visual people have a high preference for sight/vision when it comes to learning, teaching and decision making.

They tend to:

- use words relating to vision a lot in their communication (for example, 'I see what you mean; I see where you are going with that')

- find their memory is at its strongest when they can see the words, pictures or a visual aid of what they need to remember

- have great imaginations and can picture something happening and the potential outcome

- be quite observant of what is happening around them

- be descriptive when explaining something

- remember faces rather than names (unless the people they met were wearing name badges).

Visual people learn and make decisions best when:

- their environment looks appealing

- there are minimal visual distractions or movement

- they can see exactly what is being referred to

- they can watch someone perform a task first—the more times they see it the better

- they are shown the big picture up front rather than in individual steps

- information includes screenshots

- drawn diagrams of a process or visual aids are used

- they are shown how to do something or how something works.

The visual side in us can completely change the way we feel. I have a high visual modality and when the sky is bright blue, it instantly makes me happy. I am naturally drawn to vivid and bright colours and I can feel my emotions completely change based solely on what I see.

Auditory

Auditory people have a high preference for sound/hearing when it comes to learning, teaching and decision making.

They tend to:

- use words relating to sound a lot in their communication (for example, 'I hear what you're saying; it sounds like you're angry')

- find their memory is at its strongest when they can hear the words or sounds of what they need to remember

- have an interest in music and learn the words to songs very easily

- enjoy listening to podcasts

- have sensitive hearing and appreciate silence/quiet

- talk through problems and repeat instructions out loud

- remember names when introduced to people.

Auditory people work and learn best when:

- their environmental noise is calm, consistent or quiet

- there are minimal interruptions as they can take longer to refocus

- they can listen to instructions or to someone explain them

- they can have a discussion or ask questions

- they are listening to a movie or recordings

- they are wearing headphones.

People with a high auditory default modality are less common than visual people. These people are drawn to sounds and usually have extremely good hearing. My husband has a very high auditory modality and my daughter has inherited this from him. They are the kind of people who can hear a song once and know the words. He can also hear the tiniest noise when we are in the car and I have many memories of him searching for what is making that noise!

Kinaesthetic

Kinaesthetic people have a high preference for touching/doing/feeling when it comes to learning, teaching and decision making.

They tend to:

- use words relating to touching/doing/feeling a lot in their communication (for example, 'I feel what you mean; I know how that feels; it feels like there is something wrong')
- find their memory is at its strongest when they can touch or have a go at doing what they need to remember
- have an interest in feeling texture and testing things out to see how they work
- be happy to do 'trial and error' until they get it right
- be 'huggers', sit or stand close to and touch other people
- like being active and showing passion/emotions
- remember names when they feel connected to someone.

Kinaesthetic people work and learn best when:

- their environment is energetic and personable
- they get along with people and feel a connection to them
- there are minimal conversation disruptions
- they can be hands on and test something out
- they can be the doer while other people explain what to do
- there are activities or interaction involved
- there are other people around them.

Highly kinaesthetic people are generally drawn to other highly kinaesthetic people. They tend to stand out in a room. Their energy is high and they are very big on touch. I know when I walk into any type of retail store, I touch things as I walk around. I can't help myself, I need to know how things feel.

Digital

Digital people have a high preference for logic, research and things that make sense when it comes to learning, teaching and decision making.

They tend to:

- use words relating to learning or logic a lot in their communication (for example, 'I understand what you mean; that makes sense; that's logical')

- find their memory is at its strongest when they can read, research and understand

- have an interest in detail: they need to know the who, what, why, when and how

- be methodical and quality may be higher than quantity

- need statistics and facts

- ask questions until they are 100 per cent sure

- take the lead rather than be led

- remember names when they can relate a memory/example/story or have had a good conversation.

Digital people work and learn best when:

- their environment is highly technical

- they can check for accuracy

- they can take a lot of notes

- research material is available

- they have the opportunity to educate and share with others
- they have time and are not on a strict deadline.

The digital side to us wants details. Those who have a high digital default are generally people with high IQs as they are constantly looking for detail to absorb and analyse.

How to identify modalities

There are many free modality quizzes available on the internet that you can use to score yourself in each modality and find out what your default modality is. Simply search for 'NLP modality quiz'.

There is another simple way to identify our default modality and that is by listening and observing. There are words we tend to use that align to our modality, so if we listen to our own words, it will give us an insight into our modality.

I use the word 'love' a lot. I would say, 'I see what you mean' rather than 'I hear what you mean'. Observe what you do when you are going to purchase something. I'm always looking for the visual and touch side. Even if I'm out for dinner, if there are pictures in the menu, I am drawn to them. If I'm explaining something to someone, I tend to draw a picture or move my hands around a lot.

When I recall a memory, I visualise it. When I'm reading a book, I'm picturing it. If I buy something from IKEA or LEGO, I'll glance at the pictures, then try to have a go at putting it together. Only if this doesn't go to plan will I read the instructions as a last resort.

When I meet someone, I'm a hugger. Did you guess it? My kinaesthetic and visual side are both extremely high. In fact, there is only a one-point difference, with kinaesthetic being my default. My auditory score is very low, which explains why I am terrible at remembering names (unless there are name tags) and why I'm really not a fan of podcasts.

We don't always have the benefit of the person in front us doing a modality quiz to understand what their modality is. Listen carefully to what they say and the stories and experiences they share, and when in doubt, ask them questions about their preferences. Identifying their modality then delivering all communication and training to match their default modality will speed up their learning, along with their ability to understand.

Emotions are contagious

With our self-awareness building and our new-found confidence, we begin to realise just how contagious our mindset can be in influencing those around us. If we believe in ourselves, others tend to believe in us as well.

It is true that all emotions are contagious. A study done by Harvard Medical School and The University of California that looked at nearly 5000 individuals over a 20-year period showed that speaking to a happy person—depending on the relationships and distance of living—can, on average, increase our happiness by 20 per cent. It goes further to say that a second-degree happy person (someone who refers to a happy person) could still increase our happiness by nearly 10 per cent and a third-degree happy person (someone who refers to someone who knows a happy person) can increase our happiness by just under 6 per cent.

When I first heard this, I was shocked! I actually thought the numbers would be higher. I am generally a pretty excitable person but even so, I really did expect the impact of a really happy person to be higher. Then I stopped and thought about it.

> We can boost our happiness, on average,
> by up to 20 per cent simply by talking
> to a really happy person.

How cool is that? No hard work on our behalf. No changing our mindset or working on our happiness levels. Imagine the cascading impact in that alone! Especially in a workplace.

It led me to the question that I get asked quite often: does a negative staff member impact the culture and team more than a positive person does? Most people assume it's the negative person, but the truth is, the emotion is irrelevant. The person with the more powerful or higher intensity emotion will influence the other person.

So if we had a person who was really negative in a team of 10 and a person who was really positive, if the negative person's negative emotions were more intense than the positive person's positive emotions, then yes, they would influence the other nine people in the team. However, if the positive person's positivity was more intense, they would be more contagious.

As leaders, and even as humans, we are drawn to negative people to try to defuse their emotions or change them into being positive. It can be a real challenge to understand what values and beliefs are driving the negativity and how to help them to want to change. We can't make people change; they have to want to change their own behaviour. All we can do is help them to become self-aware first.

On the other hand, if we focus on the positive person and support lifting the other eight people's positive emotions, they will overpower the negative person. It's very important to address any inappropriate behaviour or underperformance, but let's be careful not to dwell on the challenge of changing the negative person's mindset at the detriment of the rest of the team.

Set expectations, stick to those expectations and focus on boosting the positivity. This relates to the saying 'kill them with kindness'. It is extremely hard to be angry, mean or negative to someone who is always *genuinely* kind, friendly and positive.

What emotions are you catching? What emotions are you spreading?

Creating an ownership mindset

Now that we have our mindset under control, and we know where our values and beliefs come from and how they are driving our emotions, it's time to *own it* all.

> I was sitting with a client in our second session and within the span of a month, she had gone from being ready to start trying to fall pregnant with her partner of 10 years to now being single. The break-up had come as a complete shock, but what she said next was bigger than the shock of the break-up. She said, 'I can't believe I sacrificed 10 years of my life for him! I'm ready to be a mum and I spent 10 years with him and now I'm single and becoming a mum has been put on pause.'

I hear the word 'sacrificed' much too frequently. 'Sacrificed time with our kids to work' or 'sacrificed our career to spend time with our kids,' are very common ones. Let's make it clear right now: we don't make sacrifices in life. We make decisions based on our priorities and the potential consequences at the time. The word 'sacrifice' lacks ownership. As though we did it for someone else, it wasn't our ultimate choice, or we had to do it.

My client didn't sacrifice 10 years of her life. She chose to be with her partner because she loved him and that was her decision all along. As parents, we don't sacrifice time with our kids to work; we work because our priority lies in what we receive from working at that time and deciding that it is the best/right thing to do based on the consequences or alternative options.

Creating an ownership mindset starts by acknowledging that we make choices through our lives that have led us to this very moment. The place we live, the job we work at, the car we drive, the money in our bank, the happiness we feel. It's all come about based on our choices, which we need to own. Unless we have been physically dragged or forced to do something, it was ultimately our choice. Nothing is impossible; it comes down to how badly we want it and what choices we are willing to make. We all have the same amount of time in every day, week, month and year. The choices that we make in that time determine what we achieve.

Let me ask you: 'Why do you get out of bed in the morning?'

Our conscious mind tells us it's because we have to go to work or to attend to the kids or pets, but actually that's not true.

We don't have to go to work, and we don't have to attend to anyone or anything.

So, why do we go to work?

Again, our conscious mind tells us it's to get money to pay bills such as the mortgage, rent, food and utilities; but really, we don't have to pay these bills. We don't even need to have these bills in the first place. We can live on the street or in the bush.

Why do we need to have a roof over our head and pay these bills?

As we start moving into our subconscious mind, we move through our values and into our beliefs, telling ourselves that a roof over our head provides protection and security. Maybe not just for us, but to be responsible and provide for our family.

We can continue to go deeper into our subconscious mind, understanding why protection, security or providing for our family is important, until we land on one of our core emotions (which I talk about in detail in chapter 6) but even at this point it becomes very clear that we don't get out of bed and go to work because we have to or to get paid. We do it to meet the emotional need of protection, security or providing for ourselves/our family. When we own this decision and know our true purpose for getting up in the morning, our mindset changes, and it is a lot easier to be motivated when the emotional driver is so obvious.

This emotional driver can change at different times of our lives. When my kids were first born, my emotional driver was being with them. Work was something I did when I wasn't with them. As they got older, my career again became a higher priority. It doesn't mean my kids have become any less of a priority—of course they will always be my strongest driver—but as they get older, working longer hours or going for dinner or a drink without them becomes a higher priority. Time spent on me starts to increase in my priority list again as they become more independent and want time to themselves.

While people can tell us what to do, it is we who decide whether to do it based on our priorities and the potential consequences of not doing it. Remembering that our mind likes to be right, it also doesn't like being told what to do because it feels like it has lost control and independence. The sooner we can look at our decisions, change our language and own each and every decision we make, the sooner we'll make it through stage 1 of The EI Rewiring Process and *own it*!

Own it

- The three levels of awareness of the human mind are the unconscious mind, the conscious mind and the subconscious mind.

- Our emotions, values, beliefs, habits and long-term memory live in our subconscious mind.

- Moving through the conscious mind and into our subconscious mind allows us to understand our emotional drivers and the true purpose of everything we do.

- The only real thing we have control over in this world is our mindset and how we choose to react.

- The need to be right is embedded in our mind. Once our mindset is decided, we look for justification to prove to ourselves that the mindset we decided on was the right one.

- Our emotional response and mindset are guided by our values and beliefs, with our responses being dependent on whether a situation supports or questions these values and beliefs.

- Our modalities are the ways in which we learn, communicate and make decisions and they determine how fast and how well we take in information, which will inevitably align with our values and beliefs or create a trigger.

- The four main modalities are visual, auditory, kinaesthetic and digital.

- Emotions are contagious, with the strongest emotion being the most contagious.

- Creating an ownership mindset starts by acknowledging that we don't sacrifice. It is the choices we have made through our lives based on our priorities at the time that have led us to this very moment.

Chapter 6

Face it: Controlling our emotions and working with them

Now that we own who we are and what makes us 'tick', it's time to regulate our emotions and *face it*. This stage of The EI Rewiring Process is about facing our emotional triggers and our responses in different situations. It's about facing who we are and working with it rather than against it. It's about facing some of our greatest fears and learning to mitigate.

There's a scientific process that occurs in our emotional mind, and understanding how it works helps us develop resilience and techniques to react exactly in the way we want to, resulting in the best outcome for everyone.

Let's start by understanding our core emotions.

Core emotions

With some exceptions, research generally confirms there are between six and 12 core emotions. The number and names are not really relevant as long as we understand that there are core emotions and sub-emotions. Each emotional feeling we have falls into one of these areas.

I tend to align to eight core emotions because I believe this provides a good balance. Author Pia Mellody lists the eight core emotions as fear, guilt, passion, shame, love, pain, joy and anger, as detailed in figure 1. I really love Pia's list because she not only lists the sub-emotions for each core emotion, but she also includes the benefits that each emotion brings.

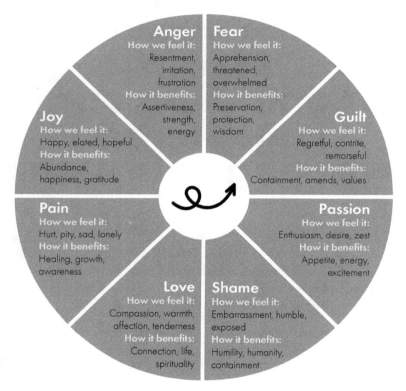

Figure 1: the y of our emotions
Source: Adapted from a list by Pia Mellody.

There are two really important things to know about emotions:

1. *There is no such thing as a bad emotion.*

    There really isn't. There is an inappropriate time and severity level for displaying each and every emotion. We naturally think that joy and being happy are good emotions. If someone is telling us something sad or bad, then displaying the emotion of joy is certainly not appropriate. If we are attending a funeral, reacting with laughter may not be appropriate. The emotion should be appropriate for the situation.

In the same way, anger is not a bad emotion. We know we are strong when we are angry. Our body physically responds to the 'fight' trigger and blood surges to our hands to give us our greatest strength. For that reason, some people channel anger when exercising or doing strenuous workouts/activities. It comes down to understanding the appropriate time to display each emotion.

Have you ever said a funny one-liner and someone laughed hysterically and you started to think ... 'ummm, it wasn't that funny'?

Or when we see road rage incidents where someone gets cut off and it quickly escalates into physical violence. Anger or frustration may have been appropriate, but maybe only a 1 out of 10 anger reaction, whereas a 9 out of 10 would have been completely overboard, indicating that the severity doesn't match the situation. This is what we mean by 'appropriate' severity levels.

I can remember when I was pregnant with our daughter and I found myself crying at a TV ad. Even a sad film clip would send me into blubbering tears. It wasn't the wrong or bad emotion to be displaying. My emotional response was exactly the emotion that the ad or film clip was looking to trigger, just maybe not at that severity level. Of course, that was my hormones taking control, but it shows that emotions certainly have severity levels that can take our emotional response from being appropriate to possibly inappropriate.

2. *We are always feeling an emotion.*

I hear a lot of people say, 'I don't want to be sad anymore' or 'I don't want to respond with anger when that happens'. The question is, 'How do you want to respond instead?' We are always feeling an emotion. We can't switch our emotions off—when we try to switch them off we default back to a previous emotion, based on the trigger, and bring on the only way we know how to react to that situation based on our memories, values and beliefs. Instead, we decide how we want to feel.

Begin by asking yourself, 'What emotion do I want to trigger in this situation?'

Recognising our emotions and triggers

A trigger is a situation or occurrence that sets off an emotional reaction in our subconscious mind. Each one of us can have hundreds of different triggers that will either align with or cause a reaction based on our memories, experiences, values and beliefs. A trigger can even be a person, based on what we think of them and our relationship with them. Identifying what the triggers are for our high-severity emotional responses is a great place to start.

In a workshop I was running I asked the attendees to think of something that makes them really angry. One gentleman put his hand up and said, 'When my wife drives our car and scrapes the hubcaps every time she pulls into the driveway!' This is a very specific example of a trigger, but also a great one to use as an example. Reason being that there is quite a lot of notice before this trigger occurs. When they first get in the car and his wife is driving, he knows that there is a high probability that this anger trigger is coming. As they turn the car into the street they live in, again he knows this possibility is coming. When he can see his house, yep here it comes ... Triggers like these are great ones to start with. We don't always have the option to see a trigger coming.

Similarly, a lady I met at a conference said her emotions are triggered when she gets on a plane and the person next to her takes both of the armrests. Again, there is so much notice of this emotion being triggered—from the day the flight is booked all the way to clicking in that seatbelt.

For other triggers, the notice period can be seconds. Especially in the workplace, where so many different people, personalities and beliefs come together. Being yelled at is an occurrence that I know triggers an emotional response in me. We don't always have a lot of notice when someone is going to yell at us, which makes this emotional response harder to regulate but extremely important to identify as the trigger of an extreme emotional response.

I've known people who are triggered by certain other people. All the other person needs to do is open their mouth to say something and they are already triggered, ready to tell them they are wrong or why what they are saying is irrelevant.

Identifying as many of our emotional triggers as possible helps us get to know ourselves on a deeper level. Triggers are driven by our core values and beliefs. The trigger is what signals our amygdala to draw on our subconscious mind and know what emotional response is required based on those values, beliefs and long-term memories.

Some people like to keep a journal or list to note down each time any high-severity emotional response is triggered in them and what it was that actually triggered the emotion. Recognising triggers and the core emotion that they activate is the first step towards regulating and controlling our emotions.

Reframing our emotional response

Reframing our emotional response is what I believe, by far, to be the toughest part of emotional intelligence to learn and master. Changing how we respond emotionally to a situation takes time, and a lot of practice. Once we have recognised our trigger, we can then decide how we want to respond.

So, if we don't want to be angry, what do we want to be?

Sometimes the core emotion might stay the same; however, the severity level will decrease. Instead of being a 9 out of 10 angry, I want to only be a 3 out of 10 angry. Remembering that whenever there is a scale or goal, it's not a matter of going from a 9 out of 10 to a 3 out of 10 overnight. It is understanding what I can do to turn that 9 out of 10 into an 8 out of 10, then to a 7, then a 6, and so on.

Asking ourselves what value, belief, memory or experience is driving this emotional response is challenging; however, it is a much-needed understanding.

Ask yourself: 'Do I want to change this? Why do I want to change this?' What stands to happen if I don't change this? 'What stands to happen if I don't change this?

What we stand to gain from changing our emotional response has to be more than what we stand to lose. Everything we do in life is a 'What's in it for me?'

Even when we think we are doing it for someone else, we are actually doing it for the emotional feeling it gives us from doing something for someone else. There has to be a personal benefit to changing the emotional response and most importantly, we have to want to change and achieve that emotional outcome.

How do your current responses make you feel? Why is this a problem?

It takes review, self-awareness, owning our response and calling ourselves out on our behaviour until we change a habit and effectively reframe the trigger. This takes time and practice. I teach EI and there are still times when I am triggered and I start to respond, only to stop myself, thinking, 'That's not very emotionally intelligent.' EI takes review and practice!

Let's continue with the example of the gentleman whose wife always scraped the hubcaps of their car when pulling into their driveway. After having attended my workshop and learning about self-awareness and emotional responses, the first time this happened again the gentleman may have become aware of his anger shortly after he became angry. The next time (because it is highly likely it will happen again) it might have been as his anger kicked in. The following time (yes, it's happened again), self-awareness might have started as the blinker went on and the car was pulling into the driveway. Then, self-awareness might have occurred even sooner, as the car turned into his street or as his wife got in the driver's seat of the car. With reflection, repetition and review, eventually we can plan for the trigger knowing it is very likely to present itself and we reframe and create a new memory/belief/value to embed.

The mistake we often make is trying to remove the circumstance that creates the trigger, or hoping it won't happen again. We are never going to stop everything that triggers our emotions from happening.

Accepting that something is going to happen and that the only thing we can control is how we choose to respond is where EI comes in.

Stopping the gentleman's wife from driving the car is not emotionally intelligent—it's avoidance. Owning his own emotional reaction and triggers based on his values and beliefs, then working with rather than against them, is being emotionally intelligent.

For those circumstances where we don't have a lot of notice, pausing and taking a deep breath allows our mind to process the information and get deeper into our subconscious mind. This provides us with time to decide exactly what emotional response we want to deliver and how we will deliver it.

Emotional hijack

When our emotions are triggered, a scientific process takes place in our mind that can lead us to 'emotional hijack'. Figure 2 shows the standard process of information being received through our five senses: sight, hearing, taste, smell and touch.

The information is first sent to our thalamus, which converts it into a language that the brain can understand. Then it heads to the neocortex, which processes the information and decides what type of response is required, sending that on to the amygdala, which sends the emotional response through our body.

I love the physical response our body has with each emotion: fear sends a surge of blood to our legs giving us the power to run as fast as we can; shock widens our eyes to extend our peripheral vision as much as possible to take everything in quickly. It's fascinating how the emotional response that is triggered also creates a physical response throughout our entire body.

There is a dotted line in figure 2 (overleaf) between the thalamus and the amygdala. This represents the path of an emotional hijack.

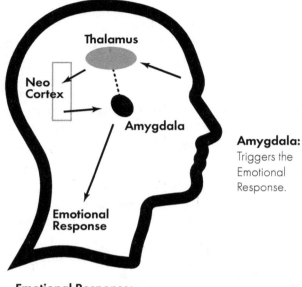

Thalamus:
Converts into brain language.

Neo Cortex:
Processes visual information and assesses what type of response is required. Signal sent to Amygdala for Emotional Response.

Thalamus

Neo Cortex

Amygdala

Amygdala:
Triggers the Emotional Response.

Emotional Response

Emotional Response:
Blood pressure, muscles, and so on.

Figure 2: emotional hijack

Emotional hijacking occurs when information has come in via our senses to our thalamus, but before it can be sent to our neo cortex (where our logic sits) to be analysed and understood, it follows the dotted line straight to our amygdala. This is what causes us to react emotionally before we have processed information—that is, we go into what is referred to as an 'emotional hijack'.

In January 2019, I was with my husband and two kids camping in Busselton, Western Australia, at our favourite caravan park. We had been staying at this same park, with another family, for more than six years so the kids knew it really well and had made friends there.

Our daughter Amelia, who was 12 at the time, had been swimming in the pool with a friend for a couple of hours and we were relaxing with our friends having an afternoon drink when we heard her scream. Somehow parents can tell their own children's screams even if they are in a room with 100 other screaming children. My husband, Mark, and I jumped up and started running towards the pool area.

At this point, all we had was information through one sense: our ears. We couldn't see her; we just knew that she was screaming. As we were running towards the pool, Mark's emotional response had him panicking and he found himself yelling 'Amelia, stop screaming!' Of course, she didn't. (I don't think any child has every stopped screaming because they were told to stop screaming!) I, on the other hand, had emotional hijacks going crazy in my brain. Here's what was going through my mind:

Fear: 'Oh my goodness, what is happening to her?'

Fear: 'Is she dying? What state are we going to find her in?'

Guilt: 'What kind of mother am I letting my daughter play in the pool without me watching?'

Shame: 'If she needs to go to hospital, I can't even drive her because I've been drinking!'

My emotional hijack jumped from fear to guilt to shame within seconds.

As soon as I reached the gate, I could see Amelia walking. I received more information through another sense: my eyes. Seeing her walk and all of her limbs intact eased some of my fear. I could see her face was covered in blood and I now knew where the main injury was. With this information going to my thalamus, through my neo cortex then on to my amygdala, my emotional response changed again. Love and compassion kicked in as I comforted her, asked her if she was okay and took her to get cleaned up.

It turned out that as Amelia was coming up from under the water, another girl jumped in with her knees tucked up and Amelia received a knee to her nose, resulting in a broken nose. She was okay in the end, and the poor little girl who jumped in, and her mum, felt terrible and came to check on her several times.

Emotional hijacks like this happen every day. We have blood taken, then receive a call from the nurse asking us to come in and see our doctor about the results. No, they can't discuss the results over the phone ... instant emotional hijack. My friend was convinced she was dying following one of these calls. She had a very long, restless night after searching the internet for every possible symptom, only to find out the next day that everything was okay.

Ever had that moment at work when your leader walks up to you at 4.30 pm and tells you they want to have a chat in the morning, then leaves the office?

All night we are trying to think what it could possibly be about and we start overanalysing everything we have said or done, then turn up to the meeting the next morning only to find that the chat was about nothing of particular importance.

Some of us only need to hear the word 'restructure' and we start trying to work out how we are going to make repayments on that car we just bought or even put food on the table. For others, a person who annoys or frustrates us only needs to open their mouth to say something and we are ready to disagree or tell them why they are wrong.

Emotional hijacks are extremely common and it's important to remember that this is a process that naturally occurs in our mind. Lack of information can be responsible, as can anything that triggers our emotional reactions.

To disrupt an emotional hijack, information becomes key. Most hijacks occur due to a lack of information, so providing or accessing more information enables our mind to process and analyse things in order to avoid or resolve the hijack. In addition to information, self-regulation of any preconceived beliefs may be required.

Recognising when and why these emotional hijacks happen to us, and to the people around us, is paramount in disrupting the hijack.

Sensory overload

In addition to emotional hijacks, we can also find ourselves in sensory overload. Sensory overload is when one or more of our five senses receive too much stimulus simultaneously and we become completely overwhelmed. It tends to become all too much and triggers our coping mechanisms.

Simple sensory overload can occur on a regular basis. If I walk into a shop that has a lot of stock in it or is extremely unorganised, the methodical and organised part of my mind struggles. My high kinaesthetic side knows that there is far too much to touch in there and my visual side struggles with how I'm going to see everything ... So I start in one corner and work my way around.

In some circumstances, it's all too much and I will turn around and walk straight back out as it creates sensory overload and it's completely lost me. Rarely do I shop in department stores for this reason.

I've heard many people say they feel like this, for example, with some websites being too 'busy' or even walking into a house that has a lot of knick-knacks or clutter.

For companies, having too many products or too many choices on the table can create sensory overload for the customer, who will walk away rather than having to make a decision. Highly digital people, however, are in their element!

There are also extreme days when there is far too much loud noise or too many people or too many problems/challenges. Highly auditory people can struggle with too many different noises occurring at the same time. Our mind goes into overwhelm and literally cannot cope with the level of detail and information. We've all had these days at some point.

To deal with sensory overload, we reduce the number of senses that are being activated at any one time. I take time for myself where no-one is talking to me and I don't need to actively listen or talk. My ultimate escape is doing a jigsaw puzzle with café jazz music on in the background. It's purely a background noise that doesn't require me to listen, yet it's calming to my mind so I'm not overthinking. The puzzle only requires me to find matching colours or pieces so I'm not having to be analytical or learn and take in something. I love reading books, but this doesn't work in this instance because I have no room left in my mind to comprehend reading.

We just want to limit the use of as many senses as possible and preferably limit the people interacting with us. Other people can be in the room but just not in our head.

Next time you experience sensory overload, try limiting some of your senses and the use of your mind to learn or process. Give yourself a chance to wind down and effectively reset all of your senses, your emotions and your mind.

Conscious and unconscious bias

As I was writing this book, I received a call from a friend who doesn't have a great relationship with her manager. They really aren't seeing eye to eye at the moment. She told me about an incident where she tabled an idea in a team meeting only to be ignored and then spoken over by her manager. The following week her manager tabled the same idea, noting that an external consultant had mentioned it and she thought it was a great idea. The team were silent and shocked, recalling what had happened at the previous meeting.

This example showed that before she had even spoken, her manager had already decided that my friend wasn't going to be saying anything of value. This was based on past triggers, memories, experiences and embedded beliefs. It was also an example of conscious bias as the manager was very aware that she was making that decision. The manager presumably reconsidered the idea at a later time and decided it actually was a great idea, but her pride and conscious bias insisted that recognition was pointed elsewhere.

Unconscious bias may also have played a role if her mind really did block out the memory and the idea, reframing it in a totally different context. In other words, due to unconscious bias when she heard the idea from someone else, it was like a completely different idea that she was hearing for the first time!

Conscious and unconscious bias are created based on our current beliefs and values. These beliefs or values then form the trigger that creates an emotional reaction driven by embedded bias rather than an open mind based on the information presented at the time. In some cases, an emotional hijack is caused based on the overall bias.

Identifying our triggers for highly emotional responses can help to bring to light embedded bias and when it is occurring. Reframing the bias and the trigger rather than responding reactively should proactively reduce the emotional hijacks.

Smashing through fear and self-doubt

Some of the greatest emotional hijacks involve fear. Fear is one of the biggest blockers for holding us back and limiting our ability. Remember, though, that fear isn't a bad emotion. We need fear. If we didn't have fear, we would die. Fear gives us limitations that stop us from doing things that are dangerous or could ultimately kill us. Without fear, what would stop us from jumping off a building and trying to fly, or running into fire? It's fear that creates the limitations required for our safety.

There are times when some people could do with a little more fear. Being overtaken by someone on the freeway doing 15 kilometres over the speed limit makes me think they could do with a bit more fear.

Picture fear as if it were a vortex surrounding us. For some of us, that vortex might be, say, 30 centimetres away from our body, whereas for others it might be 3 metres away. Everybody's fear vortex is different: it's like a big rubber band that stretches in and out depending on the situation.

I may have a fear of clowns, while other people might be completely fine with them. I may be okay with spiders and others might be petrified of them. Our fear changes based on the circumstances we are in, with our vortex stretching in and out accordingly. One minute we are the bravest person in the room and the next we are the one sweating profusely huddled in the corner.

Fear can present itself as a tangible item; however, our core fear will always be a fear of the potential emotional feeling or outcome. For example, a fear of heights, snakes or spiders is most likely associated with a fear of dying. A fear of public speaking is more likely to be a fear of judgement or a fear of failure than the actual public speaking. We always fear how it will make us feel and the emotional outcome should the worst-case scenario actually happen.

Fear of failure, fear of uncertainty (lack of control) and fear of judgement are some of the most common fears in all of us. Failure tends to be linked to the need to be successful and right. Our mind is programmed through our younger years to succeed in life and it is wired to believe we will be rewarded when we are right. Think about our schooling years: each grading, exam, question ... It's all about getting the right answer. So when we are faced with not getting the outcome that we were planning or hoping for, that feeling of failure or getting it wrong comes over us.

Fear of uncertainty aligns to our mind's need for answers and to plan. If we don't know why something happened or what is coming next, we can't plan and process it. Without that we have a lack of control and our natural defence, or fear (fight or flight) instincts, kick in.

Fear of judgement is our human-to-human connection and the desire to be liked. We are naturally drawn to other people and we like to be liked. It makes us feel like good people when other people like us or agree with us—again linking back to the need to be right. Happy emotions trigger chemicals in our brains and people showing care, liking us or loving us helps to trigger these chemicals.

We find that most people only have one or two core fears, yet fear presents itself in so many different ways.

Facing fear

I had a client, Mary, who had a fear of diving into water, a fear that I hadn't come across before. We spoke about the fear to try to understand where it had come from and how to smash through it.

By posing a series of questions and following the process outlined below, I encouraged Mary to face her fear.

If you have a fear, feel self-doubt or have a decision to make, use the following steps and questions to smash through it.

1. Identify the fear

Fear is a level of self-doubt that is created by our minds based on our beliefs. It only exists because it has been embedded in our beliefs and we truly believe it.

What fear is actually driving you? Where did it come from? What is the embedded belief? What value is keeping it in place?

Mary struggled to work out where her fear came from. She couldn't remember a time when she wasn't afraid of diving into water. The belief was that if she tried to dive in, it would be a disaster because she really didn't know how to dive properly. There was no real value in keeping her fear in place because it caused limitations, and Mary certainly wasn't gaining anything by not being able to dive. In fact, she wanted to smash through this fear.

This is paramount when we're going through this process: we have to *want* to smash through the fear. It's okay to keep a fear in place if that's what we want to do. Don't ever feel like you have to change yourself or you have to clear a fear. If you are comfortable for that fear to remain in place, then keep it. Simple!

> There are times when there is value or what we call a 'third gain' in keeping a fear or self-doubt in place. I read a case study where a lady in her forties had a right-knee reconstruction and was in her six-week recovery period. During that period, her teenage kids and husband cooked dinner each night and kept the house in order. Her sister brought her flowers and stopped in to see her most days.
>
> On her six-week check-up, her specialist spoke to her about her recovery progress not being where it should be. She genuinely wanted to recover but there was a 'third gain' or value in staying as she was. It was the first time in a long time that she had had so much rest, so much help around the house and had seen so much of her sister.

At times, our subconscious mind can do the same thing with a fear or self-doubt. If there is something to gain in keeping that fear or self-doubt in place, our subconscious mind can influence the outcome in order to protect that value and 'third gain'. This is not always the case with every fear or some areas of self-doubt; however, it is definitely worth assessing whether there is something to gain deep down that is blocking the outcome.

2. What's the worst-case scenario?

Fear creates uncertainty and loss of control. Being able to identify the worst-case scenario, and any other possible scenarios, then present our mind with the possible options and it feels like it has more control even though it doesn't know the outcome.

So, what is the outcome that you fear the most? What is the worst thing that could possibly happen?

This is what creates the fear in the first place. It's not really about the action, it's about the emotional outcome.

What would that lead to? What is the underlying core emotion?

During our conversation, I said to Mary, 'What if we went to a pool right now and you had to dive in? If you didn't have a choice—it was 100 per cent going to happen? Picture yourself standing on the edge of the pool and diving in right now. What is the worst thing that could possibly happen?

Mary looked straight at me and said, 'People would laugh at me. They would see how bad I was; how silly I looked; and they would laugh, point and comment how ridiculous I looked.'

Right then, we had found the core fear. The fear of judgement.

3. When else did you have this fear?

Now that we had found the core fear of judgement, it was time to understand when this fear had occurred before. I asked Mary, 'What happened then? What was driving it? Did you overcome it? How did you overcome it?'

As Mary and I talked more about how her fear of judgement stopped her from jumping into water, we identified that it sometimes also happened in the office. Mary was in a senior leadership position and was the youngest by quite a few years. There was an underlying fear of judgement whereby Mary felt that the other senior leaders might be questioning her ability, experience and decisions at times.

There wasn't anything specific that had led to her believing this, but it was definitely present more times than she would have liked it to be.

The more we spoke, the more times we identified the fear of judgement presenting itself in her life in quite a few different circumstances. Mary couldn't think of any specific times when this fear had been present and she could remember overcoming it. But she was absolutely ready to overcome it now.

4. What's my need?

Smashing through any type of fear or self-doubt starts with mitigation.

How do you either limit or mitigate the risk from occurring? What would need to happen for this not to be a problem? What beliefs would you need? What training or skills? What emotions would you need? What do you physically need?

I ran through these questions with Mary to better understand what her need was. A lack of confidence in herself and not knowing that her peers also had confidence in her were the biggest barriers holding her back. Confidence is not something that can be purchased, nor is it a training course that can be done in a day.

Confidence is in our mindset and our subconscious mind requires information in order to build this confidence. There was nothing specific that Mary's peers had said or done that was contributing to this lack of confidence or the reason for the fear of judgement. It was 100 per cent in Mary's thoughts so in order to change these thoughts, her mind needed more information that would override the current state.

5. Let's do it

Once we get to the 'let's do it' stage, we have analysed what the fear is, where it came from, what is the worst-case scenario and what we need in order to smash through it. This final step lies completely in our own hands. It's time to commit to doing what is required to smash through this fear.

What is the easiest way to solve this? What is the hardest way to solve this? What is the quickest way or the longest way? How would you feel if you solved this? Do you want to feel like that? What is the first step to making this happen? What could you do right now?

Our mind is naturally always looking for the quickest and easiest way to solve any problem. If there isn't a quick, easy way, we often find ourselves saying, 'It's impossible' or 'It can't be done'. There is no such thing as impossible. It simply comes down to how badly we want it and what we are willing to do in order to achieve it. We will look at the emotional undertone of the words 'it's impossible' in chapter 8.

The easiest and quickest way for Mary to break through the fear of diving into water is to go straight to the pool and dive in again and again and again until she improves her diving technique and, more importantly, to look around to see that no-one is laughing or really cares.

However, solving the fear of diving into water isn't going to solve the fear of judgement appearing in other areas of her life. For that it requires her to build her overall confidence in who she is.

In the workplace, the easiest and quickest way is to provide the information that her mind needs to build confidence and override the fear of judgement. She is looking for positive feedback from her peers showing their confidence in her ability. This will resolve the situation now, but will only fix it for the workplace and with those specific people. It won't smash through her fear of diving in water and if her peers change, a new peer may open up the possibility of her fear returning.

The hardest and longest way is to build Mary's own confidence in herself and her ability. While this is not a quick fix, it is a long-term fix. This will then resolve each situation where fear of judgement is evident and will also build Mary's overall confidence.

The thought of achieving this outcome absolutely lit up Mary's face. She was well and truly ready to feel like this and wanted to start in the workplace—diving into pools was now a lower priority.

What would it take for Mary to feel confident in herself? Mary identified three areas that would assist in building her confidence.

The first was to attend a leadership/business course. 'I don't know what I don't know.' Mary felt that if she attended an extensive program she would gain confidence in what she knew and the areas in which she had to grow.

The second area to address was in relation to her performance. She was sure that she was doing well, and that people were benefitting and growing from her skills, but she couldn't be completely sure. Mary organised to receive 360-degree feedback from a selection of staff members. Half were ones she had strong relationships with, and the other half were people with whom her relationship could be stronger. Her peers would be included in these groups.

The third area was having an internal mentor who could see her in action and provide timely feedback on situations. Mary had a strong relationship and a lot of respect for the CEO. He was the perfect person to provide specific feedback and guide her in developing her confidence and skills within the senior leadership team.

Even just putting these three initiatives in place helped Mary with her mindset. Giving our subconscious mind more information can make it feel like it has more control because answers, and the why behind them, are what our mind craves. Along with information, Mary now had actions. When there is something for us to actually do, it gives us a feeling of more control over the situation and the outcome.

* * *

Fear will always have the ability to creep in when we least expect it. Like any part of EI, it's about learning the tools and processes to go through because every situation is different, just as every person is different. If we are committed and truly want to smash through fear, we always have the power to do it.

Our own mind is what created fear and our own mind is the only thing that can smash through it.

The only things we have control over in this world are ourselves and our mind.

Owning and facing this means we can comfortably get out of our own head and start to feel for others.

Face it

- *Face it!* is about regulating our emotions and facing our emotional triggers and our responses in different situations.

- There is no such thing as a bad emotion; it all comes down to the appropriateness of the emotion and the severity level.

- We are always feeling an emotion — every second of the day — so we can't just turn our emotions off. If we don't like the way we are feeling or reacting, we must decide how we want to feel instead.

- A trigger is a situation or occurrence that sets off an emotional reaction in our subconscious mind.

- Recognising our triggers and the core emotion that they activate is the first step towards regulating and controlling our emotions.

- Reframing our emotional response is a process of reviewing, self-awareness, owning our response, deciding how we want to react instead and calling ourselves out on our behaviour until we change the habit and effectively reframe the trigger.

- Emotional hijacking occurs when we react emotionally to information before we have had time to process it. The logical mind is not involved and we are reacting without analysis and led by emotions.

- Sensory overload is when one or more of our five senses receive too much stimulus simultaneously and we become completely overwhelmed.

- Conscious and unconscious bias are based on our current beliefs and values, which form the trigger that creates an emotional reaction driven by embedded bias.

- Fear is a level of self-doubt that originates in our minds and is based on our beliefs. We are the only ones who can create our fears and we are the only ones who can challenge and disrupt them.

Chapter 7

Feel it: **Understanding others and the impact we have on them**

A couple of years ago, I was hired by a large financial institution that was experiencing an increase in escalations and complaints reaching middle and even senior management. The senior exec team was concerned about why this was happening.

They had an active process with clear options for dealing with client complaints and the power to make quick decisions on solutions where appropriate.

We sat down and reviewed the process. They had put a lot of thought into it. If there was an error on their behalf, teams were empowered to waive up to a set financial amount, with their team leads having a slightly higher authority limit. The staff were encouraged to defuse the situation as quickly as possible while remaining professional and in solution mode.

After listening to a few of their recorded calls with customers, it was obvious that they had skipped the vital and most powerful step: empathy.

Empathy: the greatest skill of all

If we think back to those people in our lives who inspire us or who have left the biggest positive impact on us, we will notice that most of them have one skill in common: empathy. It is often confused with sympathy, but there is a big difference between the two.

Sympathy is feeling sorry for someone. It's understanding the situation they are in, genuinely feeling sorry that they are in it and having to go through it.

Empathy is recognising the emotional response someone is having and being able to understand how it feels to have that emotional response.

I hear a lot of people refer to empathy as 'putting yourself in their shoes'. This is fraught with danger. When we put ourselves in someone else's shoes, judgement comes with it. We might not agree with how they are reacting, or we might be thinking, 'I'd never do that'. This judgement makes it hard for us to understand the situation and, most importantly, the other person's emotional reaction.

To display empathy, or be empathetic, we don't need to know what has happened. All we need to do is recognise the emotion and the severity of the emotion the person is feeling. What caused that emotion is irrelevant.

There are three steps to empathy: recognise, recall and respond. If we were to walk into a room and be confronted by someone who is extremely angry, we wouldn't need to know what made them angry to show empathy. *Recognising* the emotion—extreme anger—is the first step.

The second step is to *recall* the last time we were extremely angry. It doesn't matter what the situation was or what caused our anger.

The last time you felt extremely angry, what would have been the worst thing somebody could have said or done to you and what was the best thing they could have said or done?

When we are confronted with an extremely angry person, our natural *response* is to try to defuse the situation. The first thing that may come to mind is to say, 'Calm down' or 'It's not that big of a deal'. We may even try to resolve the problem straight away by telling them how easy it is to fix. Providing a 'quick-fix' solution can cause frustration and make us feel like we are being shut down and overreacting.

By recalling the last time we were extremely angry, we may realise that the worst thing someone could have said to us is, 'Calm down'—that would be downplaying the situation and our emotions.

This would also be the case if we are extremely happy or joyful—we wouldn't want someone telling us not to be so excited or to calm down.

Whenever we are feeling any form of high-severity emotion, the first thing we want is to be heard. We want to let the emotion out and for someone to listen to why we are feeling so emotional.

Showing empathy, or being empathetic, isn't rocket science, but it does take a bit of mind disruption for us to think differently from how our natural response would like us to.

Our natural response would be to try to defuse any negative, confrontational or high-severity emotion that we are not comfortable with. It's about getting completely out of our own head and understanding the emotion and what the person needs from us.

The large financial institution I was working with was skipping the empathy step and going straight into solution mode. This was making their customers feel like they were overreacting, that their emotions were potentially not warranted, and that they didn't feel listened to. It's like having a conversation with someone who gives you a reason why every answer you come up with won't work.

You could say the sky is blue and they would tell you why it's not. Their defence mechanisms are up, logic is not playing a part in it and their emotions have taken over.

How would you communicate in a way that displays empathy?

Delivering empathy

Any tough conversation can be made a whole lot easier if we are empathetic. The ultimate purpose is to help the other person gain control of their emotions and feel a connection.

Here are five easy steps for being empathetic and handling any tough conversation.

1. Listen and ask open questions

We are there to listen. Let the other person get all of the emotion out that they need to. Do not interrupt; just listen. Ask open questions when required to help them continue talking. We will know when they have finished talking because they will ask us a question.

I hear from so many clients how they receive a phone call and the customer is angry and yells at them before asking to speak to a manager. By the time they speak to the manager, they are no longer as angry and everything is settled. This happens because when we are in an emotional state, we want to let it all out straight off and unfortunately the first person we talk to tends to hear all of our emotions at their peak.

2. Acknowledge and pause

Acknowledging the emotion doesn't have to be about agreeing with the emotional response. It is simply ensuring that we have read the emotion the other person is feeling correctly. If the emotion is clearly obvious, this part of the step may not be needed.

We also want to acknowledge what has happened and the circumstances, especially if we are in any way at fault. With this acknowledgement we are validating their emotions. Again, we don't have to agree with the emotion; we are simply validating the cause and response. It's showing the person in the emotional state that we understand how they are feeling and have understood what they are saying.

I already briefly spoke about the benefits of pausing in chapter 5. In this circumstance, the other person is already in their subconscious mind, which is where the emotion is coming from. The pause at this step is to ensure they have said everything they want and need to say. Cutting them off or interrupting creates a defence response. Remember: we will know they have finished speaking when they ask us a question.

3. How do we fix this?

Once it is obvious that they have finished speaking, we are ready to go into solution mode. When we are in a highly emotional state, it is generally because the outcome that we expected didn't occur. The majority of people in this state already know how they want it fixed. They already know what they wanted to happen because it didn't happen, which is what made them respond in this emotional way. They know what they want to happen now. They also want us to take a role in the ownership.

At this stage, we ask them, 'How do we fix this?' The 'we' in this question is extremely important. It instantly creates an equal stature: we are in this together. It is also asking the other person how they want this to play out. What solution do they have in mind? Importantly, we are avoiding pointing the finger and saying 'you', as in, 'How do *you* want *me* to fix this?' or 'What do *you* want *me* to do?' Even saying, 'I'm going to do this' can create a stature that we are higher because we are the ones with the solution. I talk about the emotional undertone of words in more detail in chapter 8.

One of the recorded calls I listened to from the large financial institution I was working with, had the employee offering monetary compensation for an error. They were willing to waive payment for the month and were offering it like it was a prize, as though the customer should be happy with that. The customer responded by telling them, 'You can't buy your way out of this!' All the customer wanted was someone to take ownership of the error and genuinely say sorry. They wanted the employee to understand exactly how they were feeling and the emotion that their error had caused.

> Money is not an emotional driver — it is a means to an end and that end will always be an emotional feeling.

4. Actions

List and confirm the actions that will be taken, committing to a time frame and ownership. This sounds too simple, but these actions spoken out loud and then delivered as promised show ownership and alignment.

A sure way to trigger the emotion on a higher severity level is to not do what we said we are going to do. Following through with commitments is crucial and keeping the other person up to date with progress, or even communicating a lack of progress, will keep the situation in order.

5. Support

Say, 'What else can I do to help?' Avoid saying, 'What else do you need from me?' The 'you' and 'me' separate the relationship again. Offering this last step of support gives the other person the chance to review the situation in their mind. It gets them to stop and think, 'Am I happy with this? Is there anything else I want in this situation?' They own the decision and have control of the situation. It triggers a change in emotion and is like closure, looping the conversation back together and closing the initial emotion with a sense of resolve.

* * *

Never underestimate the power of empathy and emotions. Everything in this world was created for a human emotion. Every product, every industry, every need. When the emotion becomes extreme or is triggered, the key way to resolve the situation is to focus on the emotion. Empathy is the key differentiator between leaders and great leaders.

Becoming a leader

Leadership is not a title. I have heard this from many people, and it is absolutely true. While some people have the word 'leader' in their title, it certainly does not make them a leader. Vice versa, some of the greatest leaders don't have leader in their title. Too often we see people move through technical roles and climb the corporate leader, ending in a leadership position. They are extremely talented from a technical point of view but don't quite cut it as a leader. In fact, some are terrible leaders.

I've worked with some extremely intelligent people over the years who found themselves in a leadership role and became extremely unhappy. The people side of things frustrated them, and they didn't enjoy it at all. The team that respected them as a technical expert began to really dislike them as a leader. It impacted on their reputation, their mindset and their enjoyment for what they did. So often we mistake success as reaching that top job in the organisational structure rather than understanding our core skills and what makes us happy.

Leadership requires core skills and, most importantly, great EI. When we first enter into a leadership role, training in leadership skills and developing our EI are essential for becoming a flexible and adaptable leader. We would never dream of putting someone in a technical role without training, yet too often people are put in leadership roles without leadership training.

Those who can build leadership skills and their EI without it requiring a job title are the most inspirational and successful people—remembering that the ultimate success is being happy.

New leaders, or those building their leadership skills, tend to go through three stages:

1. my 'y'
2. their 'y'
3. future 'y'.

Stage 1: my 'y'

When we are first promoted to a leadership role or make the decision to be a great, aspiring leader, we can be very stuck in our own mind.

> I remember my first taste of a leadership role working for an insurance company in their customer service department. I was a fresh 24-year-old who became the senior and 2IC (second-in-charge) in a team of 10. I was so proud of my achievements and my new job title. I found myself feeling the need to prove my worthiness to my peers, my leader and even to myself. I was set on showing that I was the

> right person for the job: *I do belong around this table; Yes, I am good enough to do this; I can take control; Here's how good I am.* I was only interested in 'me' and was really stuck in that 'Own it' and 'Face it' mindset.
>
> I was making sure everyone was productive so that we could bring the workflow under control. I wanted our team to have the best results and that competitive side came out in me. I felt the need to change who I was and push the people around me to work hard.
>
> Little did I know that my reputation was being impacted and the team members were getting frustrated with me and my attitude. I was so stuck in my own head that nothing else mattered other than me being the best 2IC in the department and shining.

All leaders tend to go through this first stage of leadership where it is all about us and proving to our peers and our seniors that we are the right person for the job. Some of us spend way too much time there and sadly some of us never make it out of stage 1 — my 'y'.

Thankfully, it didn't take me long to realise that leadership is all about the people around you being happy and succeeding. If they are happy, motivated and succeeding, then we are all successful. If the team aren't happy and motivated, then no-one is successful.

We can't be great leaders without our team being happy and successful. Leadership is not about us at all. Leadership is all about leading others to be the best version of themselves they can be. It means taking a back seat at times and focusing on them and their 'why'.

Stage 2: their 'y'

Once I realised that being a leader is all about those around me, I really started to build my leadership skills in the 'Feel it' stage.

My focus moved from proving myself and my own ability to putting the team first in all circumstances — really understanding who they were, what made them tick and what their motivations were. Bringing empathy in at this stage to help identify the emotional driver for each situation and each person. My number one focus became helping each team member to develop and to find what naturally motivated them—what was their 'why'?

> Some years ago, I was working in an office with a leader who was still stuck in stage 1. It was coming up to performance and pay review time, which happens to be one of the most challenging times for a leader. At times it's like trying to share water from a small bucket that has a hole in it.
>
> This leader had a small team and a few of her staff members were quite underpaid. She came to me for advice on the best way to put together a business case to her leader to rectify the situation for these staff members. I checked in with her after the review process only to find out that she used those tips to argue a pay rise for herself first and didn't get a chance to even speak about her team members because her leader ended the conversation. It was extremely disappointing to hear.
>
> Had she understood that her leadership skills would have been on display if she had put her team first and done what she could to focus on them before thinking of herself, not only would her team have been happier and felt recognised, but it would also have shown her leader her leadership skills. It was a tough lesson to learn.

Stage 2 is all about putting our team first: What are their needs? How can I support them? What type of leadership do they need from me?

Anything that puts us last and makes the main focus all about our teams shines a light on our leadership skills and usually becomes the recipe for success for all.

Stage 3: future 'y'

If leadership is about developing those around us to be the best they can be, at some stage we are likely to do ourselves out of a job. Thinking that we are good leaders, that we are indispensable, or that the team cannot survive without us is actually the opposite of success as a great leader. That moment when we walk out of a room or workplace and everything falls over is not the time to wear it like a badge.

We know that we have succeeded as leaders when each team member has grown, is empowered and is performing at their highest ability. When our successor is knocking on our door ready to step up and lead the team.

> I really struggled with this the first time it happened. I was managing a small team for two years and they were doing very well! Work was being managed well and up to date, and we were on top of the leader board in most areas. Growth was evident, and everyone was pretty happy. I found myself starting to scratch around for work on some days.
>
> Now, there is always more to do: there are more places to take the team and more challenges to create. The bar can always be lifted. My main focus was on leadership and I felt like I'd done everything I could for this team of people for now. They no longer needed my skills. The 2IC was ready to give it a go and I needed a new challenge. It was time to move on.

This is stage 3—when we realise that we have led the team far enough and they are ready to step up to the next level, whether that is in our role or in a different team or company.

The question to ask yourself at this point is, 'Am I still learning, growing and being challenged?'

I've heard CEOs talk about their expiry date being five years. That after five years of running a company, it is time to move on and give someone else with a different style a turn. I love so much about this. Given how different we all are, a fresh set of eyes will always bring a slightly different approach. This is purely an example and for some people 'five years' may be '10 years', while others may not feel like they ever reach this level—and that's okay.

Being able to identify when our 'expiry date' has been reached as a leader—when we are no longer being challenged—is a great show of EI. It is not the end of our leadership path; it's simply the next chapter and there is a different team out there waiting for us and wanting our help.

Understanding what makes others 'tick'

Although we all have the same structural make-up and our bodies function in the same way, each one of us is completely different. Our likes, preferences and the way in which we work are all different. We know that this has a lot to do with our subconscious mind and how our values and beliefs guide us.

Becoming emotionally intelligent means we are able to pause, get out of our own mind and learn to understand the people around us. Our differences are a good thing. We should feel completely comfortable in what makes us different from others and we should feel even more comfortable and respectful of other people's differences.

Sometimes we hear things that really stick with us and hit home. I attended an amazing female future leaders program many years ago where the facilitator said during a conversation, 'Others are not a failed version of you.' This hit me like a sledgehammer, a semitrailer—it was a lightbulb moment like no other.

At the time, I was struggling with a leader in my office whose style was completely different from mine. I couldn't understand why she would approach things as she did. Why she would speak to people like she did, why she would send a particular email, why she would lead the way she did. At that moment, I released that she was probably thinking the exact same thing about me. *Why did I think my way was the right way? Maybe her way is better? Not doing things the way I do them doesn't mean she is a failed version of me.*

We all do things slightly differently. Appreciating these differences and leveraging them is what makes us a great success together.

An EI interaction profile (see table 2, overleaf, for an example) is a great way to get to know what makes other people tick. Understanding someone's technical ability or ability to do their job or perform specific skills is something that we are usually quite aware of. The emotional profile becomes the perfect complement to this knowledge, providing a more complete understanding of the person.

Table 2: EI interaction profile

Name:		Date:	
Motivator/emotional driver			
Values and beliefs			
Default emotional response (for example, anger, fear, confusion, concern, excitement, nervousness, frustration)			
Style of praise			
Style of feedback			
How to create connection			

The following sections will take you through the background of each of the areas in the table to assist you in completing the profile.

What is our motivator/emotional driver?

What is it that motivates us? If you wanted to get someone excited and pumped up ready to perform at their best, what is it that would motivate them?

What is your motivator—your emotional driver? What gets you out of bed each morning and in to work?

We all have different motivators or emotional drivers. Grouping everyone together and assuming that one form of motivation or team activity will give everyone motivation is not always accurate.

Some people's emotional driver for going to work could be to advance their career or earn money to travel, while others could be simply wanting to provide security for their family.

If we are trying to bring a team together to bond over a few drinks on a Friday night and one of our team members is either not a drinker or has young children they would prefer to be at home with, trying to force them to come for drinks could do the exact opposite of helping them to bond.

Finding and understanding what motivates each person and their real emotional driver for working is the core of understanding how to get the best out of them while respecting their priorities.

What are our values and beliefs?

Values can't be forced upon anyone. If we try to enforce company values on our staff, then they aren't values—they are rules. The minute those company values are put on the wall or coffee mugs and are forced on teams, they become rules. No-one can make anyone else value something. What's more, telling someone they have to value something is a recipe for disaster.

Helping people to identify their own values and beliefs, then bringing them together with the company's values is a far better way to create true emotional attachment. In the workplace, our values do need to align or complement each other, or we can end up with a difference in morals.

Understanding and respecting other people's values and beliefs creates rapport and trust. This is also important in life outside of work.

How well do you know each member of your family's and all of your friends' values and beliefs?

Default emotional responses

There are times when things happen that are beyond our control and we aren't prepared for or expecting them to happen. Most of us have a default emotional response that will take over the minute something happens.

Some people may instantly feel fear; others may get quite teary or upset; while others may be defensive or angry (as we saw in chapter 6 when we looked at Pia Mellody's eight core emotions). As leaders, understanding what the likely response to a situation will be from each person around us helps us to prepare for these situations. This reaction may be very similar to how open they are to change.

It's not a bad thing to not enjoy or to struggle with change. It's a bad thing to not understand and accept how we react to change or unexpected circumstances. Change is a given.

Some years ago an attendee of one of my seminars asked me, 'Amy, hasn't change always been around? Is it really any different these days?' He was absolutely right that change has been around forever and will continue to be around forever. But there is definitely a difference these days.

The extent of change that we see now is far greater than before. Technology allows us to make major changes more frequently. Ten years ago, we may have rolled out a change that improved a process and altered the steps for implementing it. A change to a process these days can be taking it from manual to completely automated with new technology and platforms. The changes that we see rolling out these days are more extreme and the gap between the current state and the future state is greater, making it more challenging for us to accept.

When a change or an unexpected situation occurs, being able to predict how others will react therefore gives us the ability to deliver it in a way that will achieve the best outcome for everyone.

The purpose is to get people to buy into the change and embrace it rather than push back on it. We should be focusing on people and their needs when it comes to change. If we know we will be delivering change to someone who struggles with change, we should chat to them individually beforehand, giving them a chance to process the change and ask as many questions as they like until they have the answers and information required to disrupt any emotional hijack.

Remember that emotions are highly contagious. It is best to approach the situation with flexibility rather than a 'cookie cutter' approach for everyone. In a room full of people hearing a major change for the first time, if there is someone extremely anxious or unaccepting of the change, their emotions will be contagious to others.

As a mum, a wife, a daughter and a sister, I also know how my family members will likely react in unexpected situations. This helps me to plan my approach to change and helps me to frame the communication that is required to achieve the right emotional outcome for everyone.

Style of praise

I am very much the extrovert when it comes to praise. I love to receive praise and I absolutely love to give it. Give me a stage, balloons, champagne and streamers—the 'big bang' is how I see praise at its finest. Naturally, we tend to approach praise in the way that works best for us. So, I've always gone for the 'big bang' when planning for those around me only to learn very quickly that this is definitely not everyone's preference.

> I once wanted to celebrate a fantastic achievement by one of my team members. I sent an email out to the team, copying in other leaders, to set up a morning tea to celebrate. The team member pulled me aside, horrified. She said she couldn't think of anything worse and to please cancel the morning tea. For her, praise was about recognition from the people involved but the 'big bang' approach absolutely wasn't her style.

Some leaders prefer a very subtle style of praise and mistakenly take this approach with their team. Hearing that people are disappointed about not receiving praise from their leader (or even their partner or family) makes me wonder if, while the leaders are actually really proud of them, they are not big fans of praise themselves. A high EI person will ensure they understand the type of praise the people around them like or need.

Take ownership and let the people around you know what type of praise you like and how it motivates you.

> It isn't praise unless it is delivered in a way that works for the person receiving it.

Style of feedback

Like change and praise, we all have a preferred style for receiving feedback. Some of us like it straight down the line—no sugar coating—and can instantly take it on board and course correct. Others like it softer so that they have time to process it and not take it personally. And there are many between those two extremes.

When and where feedback is provided should be determined by where the receiving person sits on this sliding scale. If we are delivering feedback to someone we know is going to struggle hearing it—who may get upset or defensive or will definitely need time to process it—then delivering it first thing in the morning is probably not ideal. Delivering it in the afternoon, then letting them process it overnight ready to catch up again first thing in the morning may be more productive. Be aware not to let them go home when they are in an unstable or concerning mental state. Ensure they are ready to process the information before you leave them to their own devices.

The whole purpose of delivering feedback is about the outcome, not the process. It's about getting a different result next time and helping the other person to change and improve. It is completely about them and therefore should be delivered in a way that works for them, not us.

How to create a connection

There are so many ways to create a connection with another person just by getting to know them. What types of hobbies or projects do they enjoy? What do they like to chat about over lunch? How do they spend their ultimate weekend? When in doubt, go with the one thing we all seem to avoid—just ask them, 'How do I get to know you?'

It's a common complaint from people that their leader doesn't really know them. My first question is always, 'Have you told them who you are and what drives you? Do they know your EI interaction profile?'

Yes, the leader should be skilled enough in EI to have worked this out, but it's not always the case. There is always a role that we play in the situation and something we can do to build a connection. Having a chat with our leader and letting them know what makes us tick and what style of leadership works best for us is a great place to start.

The relationship that any leader has with the people around them is enough to keep people in jobs that they might not love just because they are learning so much from their leader and generally like to be around them. A great leader continues to help people grow and is always looking for the best outcome for them.

> I have a good friend who is a recruiter for a very niche industry. We happened to be working in the same industry at one time and he said in a passing conversation that one of his clients had asked him to have a chat with one of my top performers to see if he would consider moving over to them.
>
> My friend told me that he would never speak to any of my staff because that crosses the line of our friendship. I stopped him and

> said, 'Please speak to my staff any time you think there is a great opportunity for them.' He looked at me like I was crazy. I explained to him that if any of my team weren't happy doing what they were doing or somebody could offer them something that I couldn't, then I would always support them in taking that opportunity.
>
> I went straight to the team member and let him know that the other company was interested in him. This was great encouragement for him and his credibility in the industry. He wasn't interested and didn't have the conversation, but it gave him a massive confidence boost.

Leadership is not about holding people back by being selfish and keeping them with us. We should never be afraid that someone might leave. It's about getting to know them and what makes them tick—what's important to them and whether they can achieve that by working for us. A skilled leader will work with them to develop them to their highest ability and will adapt their leadership style to align to their needs.

Adaptability and balance

Every leader brings something different to the table and each leader has their individual strengths and core skills. The greatest leaders have the ability to adapt their leadership style to not only what the team needs but also what each individual needs at any given time.

The 'BFF' leader

There are times when we need a friend in our leader. We need them to be able to have a good laugh, enjoy a muck-around and talk about the latest craze or hit song. I refer to this as the BFF leader, as in Best Friend Forever. Some people, especially highly kinaesthetic people, create trust and relationships with people they see as friends.

The pros of a BFF style of leadership are that we get to know our people on a deeper level. The trust is there, and it makes work more enjoyable. The culture tends to be positive and the people like being around their leader.

The disadvantage to this style of leadership is that being too close a friend can make managing people and having the more difficult conversations harder. If these conversations and the management side are not delivered, respect might be questioned.

The 'dictator' leader

The dictator leader tells people what to do and how to do it. This can also include micromanagement, where the leader has control and awareness of everything that is happening in the team. This style of leadership works really well during times of crisis when we turn to our leader in fear or are lost and we want to be told exactly what needs to be done and how to do it. It can also produce strong results and very clear direction and time frames, especially when there is a lot of work to do.

The downside to dictator leadership is that it may frustrate members of the team by creating a lack of empowerment, ownership and development for the team members. People may do what they are told due to fear rather than respect, limiting innovation, high performance and creativity. When ownership and empowerment are missing, we can become transactional and robot-like. Culture tends to take a hit for the worst.

The 'absent' leader

The absent leader spends an extended amount of time away from the team. This may be by choice or due to other commitments. The advantages to this style of leadership are that it provides the team the opportunity to step up into the leadership role and take on more responsibility. If this happens when the team are in a good place and performing well, it's a great time to test out how they perform without the leader around. Remember that we know a great leader has succeeded when they are no longer needed by their team.

The absent leader falls down, however, if the team no longer wants them because they are never there to lead and deliver to the team. A team with no leadership can also become disjointed, lack direction, perform poorly and become toxic.

* * *

While there are many different styles of leadership, the key is to understand that a great leader has the ability to adapt and balance all styles of leadership. They can recognise the needs of the individual and the situation, knowing exactly what style of leadership is needed.

For example, I've always believed in leaders having regular one-on-one meetings with team members, and that these meetings should be approached and designed based on the individual needs of team members. Some meetings may be short and to the point while others might go for an hour.

Finding the right balance for each person and adapting our leadership style to them rather than expecting them to adapt to our style supports their individuality and brings out the very best in each of them. While we all have a default style of leadership, we still need the ability to adapt to the situation and the person.

In my early twenties I had a decent-sized friendship group. We were all similar and hung out as a group quite a lot. Over the following years, the group became smaller as everyone found their feet and went in slightly different directions. Now, in my forties, I have a small handful of really close friends. They are all very different—so different that I don't ever bring my closest friends together because the only real thing they have in common is me.

As we get older, we surround ourselves with the people we need, each of whom brings something different to our lives.

We tend to contact a friend depending on the situation and our need. If I am having a really bad day or am extremely frustrated, I know exactly which friend I would call. If I have heard some fantastic news that I am really excited about, I know which friend I would call first in that moment. Each of our friends plays a different role in our lives.

What role do you play in your friends' or family's lives? If you are unsure of the answer, ask! Ask your friends, ask your family, ask your work colleagues.

Others can see strengths in us that we tend to overlook in ourselves. By noticing what kind of help others come to us for we can begin to understand their needs and what makes them 'tick'.

Everyone's a superstar at something

Sometimes it's necessary to delve deep to discover a person's passion and core skills if we want them to perform at their highest standard. When we are doing something we love and we are happy, our performance will naturally improve.

Twice now, I've been the leader of a team where one member was on a performance management plan, where a member's under-performance was being addressed and managed because they weren't delivering the minimum expectations of their role.

Each of these team members was seen as the 'problem child' — they weren't motivated and cared little about what they did and how they did it. After observing them for a month, it become evident to me that they were both highly intelligent but were both in the wrong role. The roles they had didn't leverage their core skills, and neither of them was passionate about their job roles. Their mind was driven and excited by tasks that were few and far between. No-one had worked out what really made them tick, including themselves.

To address this, I laid out clearly to them the expectations of their roles. I knew they were capable of performing their roles — it was work ethic and attitude that were missing due to their lack of interest and passion.

Keeping them on a performance management plan was not going to change this. They would pick up their performance while they needed to but sooner or later the boredom or dislike of their tasks would creep back in. Poor behaviour like this should always be called out. The sooner the better. Even if it has been happening for years and people have accepted that it's 'just who they are' — no! It should be called out and clear expectations should be set. We shouldn't stop there though.

With expectations made clear and monitored, I set about building a core skill portfolio of what they really loved doing. What does that perfect workday look like? Is it spent face to face with customers; is it resolving problems or complaints; is it researching or training; is it doing administrative work? What are their modalities? Do they align better to short, process-driven tasks or longer analytical tasks?

As I continued to build a list of core skills, it became obvious what type of role would allow them to spend most of their time doing what they loved. I was asked questions about whether this was rewarding their behaviour. The simple answer was 'no'. Their poor performance was addressed and expectations were set and monitored, but why continue to struggle to make someone do something that they clearly didn't love?

They had a choice: they could either stay and deliver outcomes consistently aligned to set expectations, or they could leave. As a leader, my role was to get the desired outcome in the best way possible. Why should I battle when I knew it would potentially be an ongoing 'round in circles' performance management battle and potentially impact those around them? The organisation had already put plenty of time and money into these staff members, so why not utilise their strengths?

We were lucky enough that both of these cases occurred in large organisations, so there were roles in other departments that ticked many of these two staff members' boxes. Both of them eventually landed internal transfers, on their own merits and with complete honesty, to other departments and went on to become high performers in their new roles.

Everyone is a superstar at something. We all have a capability and drive that aligns to our core skills and passions. Rather than trying to force someone to perform better in their existing role, we should question *why* they are aren't performing. What's stopping them from delivering? Poor performance should always be addressed and rectified but rather than fighting a rollercoaster that can go up and down for years, we should work on the core problem so everyone is a winner.

Appreciating that each person is different and has different core skills and strengths means we can build a team of people who complement one another to cover the majority of circumstances.

Building a balanced team

When building a team, we may be naturally drawn to people who are similar, especially when we're recruiting. If we already have a high performer in our team, we might go looking for a 'clone'. We hear people say, 'If only I had 10 clones of my high performer in my team, then everything would be perfect.' Having a team of the same type of people and skillset isn't the most balanced team—there will be limitations on what they can achieve and their ability to innovate.

In addition to a leader with great EI, a balanced team should have at least five different types of people: a work machine, an analyst, an innovator, a tech guru and a people lover. The balance creates the best platform to build an emotionally intelligent team.

The work machine

Every team needs a work machine! That person who smashes through the work. They have speed and are able to achieve a great deal in a small amount of time.

The first person the leader, and the team, look to when they are overloaded with work and need a hand is usually the work machine. The work machine's strength is speed and quantity but not necessarily quality. Their accuracy is impacted by their speed, but as long as the proportions are balanced and the quality is high, these people help to keep the team moving.

The analyst

The analyst is the perfect balance to the work machine. Analysts are known for their attention to detail and quality. They don't get through anywhere near as much work as the work machine does, but they balance this with their analytical skills. With the lower quantity comes very high quality.

Quite often the analyst and work machine frustrate each other. The work machine is looking at the analyst wondering why the analyst's workload is so much lower than their own. They might be complaining that the analyst doesn't do their fair share, yet the analyst is looking at the work machine and thinking, 'If you slowed down you wouldn't make so many errors that I then have to fix.'

This is why they create the perfect balance. A team full of work machines would make too many errors and a team of analysts wouldn't get through the work. We need them both and they should both be appreciated for their strengths and the roles they play in the team.

The innovator

We all know that person who questions everything that is done with 'Why?' The one who can always think of a more efficient or innovative way to do something. Yes, it will cost money and time, but it would be so much better. These innovators can drive us crazy but also keep our minds challenged and moving forward rather than getting stagnant and doing things the same way over and over because 'that's the way we have always done it'. With the pace and size of change that is currently occurring around us, innovators are where the difference comes in and are a key contributor to a successful team.

Innovators can get frustrated if they are in a team or workplace where change is not embraced and innovations are not a key focus. Not all innovation requires money and long periods of time. We can leverage these skills by helping them to chunk down their ideas into smaller increments. Naturally, we always want the ultimate solution or end goal. Helping them create the smaller wins or ways to innovate without spending money will keep them engaged and challenged, and will encourage change for all.

The tech guru

This is a double whammy and is often more than one person. One is the high-tech person everyone calls when a piece of technology or equipment isn't working. The other is the technical expert in a given field. They know everything about the product and processes. They might have been around for years, but either way are highly technically minded and respected for always having the answer. Often these people are mistaken for the choice of a leadership position; however, these high-tech experts may not have the core skills to be a great leader.

The people lover

This is the energetic, friendly person everyone is friends with who loves to have a chat, sometimes even a gossip, but people tend to trust and be vulnerable to. Their emotions are generally contagious so they may need assistance to build their self-regulation. The people lover tends to be a people pleaser and make a big impact on the culture of the team.

When we are building a team, reviewing what core skill gaps exist and getting the right balance creates opportunity. And of course, there's the absolute given of every team having a balance in diversity extending to inclusion. Always consider the value that gender, age, race, ethnicity, sexual orientation, socio-economic status, physical abilities, religious beliefs, political beliefs and other ideologies can bring to the performance of a team.

Challenging the obvious choice

When we are communicating with our team, our mind focuses on key words and our conscious mind can be very quick to respond based on these key words without us really listening and considering the best outcome for the situation or the team. If we can pause, disrupt the mind cycle and consider the less likely answer, we can really challenge people and outcomes.

I worked with a lady in her mid-forties — let's call her Ruby — who was not into any socialising outside of work, wasn't big on 'team bonding activities' and definitely wasn't interested in any R&R (reward and recognition) programs. Her natural default was pessimistic and her response to most conversations was to express why whatever was being discussed wouldn't work. Her work style was mostly aligned to that of an analyst.

We were doing a refresh of the R&R program for our department and I was asked to put someone forward for the working group. The obvious choice was my 'people lover', but instead I put Ruby forward as our representative.

My thought behind this was that Ruby was never going to buy into any new R&R program that was rolled out. There was a high possibility that she would be repetitively vocal, saying it was a waste of time, and that her attitude towards it could impact the team's attitude.

If I put her in the working group, she had no choice but to be a part of it and it would challenge her mindset. If the end result was something that she had signed off on and was onboard with, then I knew that everyone else would be too. I see these types of programs as a minimum delivery, and we can always go bigger, but to have her accepting and endorsing the minimum delivery was always going to work well for her and everyone around her.

The end result actually exceeded my expectation. Ruby became the biggest advocate of R&R and was constantly encouraging others to get involved. It turns out she wasn't against it — she had been burned by it in the past because she had felt it wasn't done fairly. Challenging the obvious and easy choice created a completely different experience and outcome.

If I was ever asked for my tech guru to go on a project to review a product or process, I would either send my innovator with them or if there was enough technical expertise already on the project, I would send my innovator alone.

Technical gurus love what they do and what they know. This can at times limit them from wanting to change as they may no longer be the expert. They are also so familiar with the way things have always been done that it might seem like they are looking through a preconceived lens. The innovator might frustrate the project team and that is exactly the reason why they should be there: to challenge them to think differently. To be a set of eyes looking from the outside in, questioning why we do it that way.

If we aren't challenged or feeling even a little awkward, are we even growing? Taking the time to pause and tap into our subconscious mind provides us with the opportunity to challenge the obvious answer and look for opportunities to really take it to the next level.

Measuring the differences

With a balanced team, high EI and leveraging of core skills and strengths, it would be crazy to expect to measure everyone against the same key performance indicators, budgets or measurements.

Can you imagine giving your work machine and your analyst the same budget or workload and expecting them to deliver the same thing? The analysts are always going to get through less work, but their quality will be higher. Appreciating and leveraging the strengths also means measuring against what you really want them to deliver. I've seen an analyst put on performance management and even let go from workplaces because their statistics weren't high enough. Equally, I've seen work machines let go because their quality wasn't high enough.

Once we have a balanced team in place, we have to ensure cookie cutter performance measures aren't being implemented that absolutely defeat the purpose of having a balanced team in the first place.

Leaders with high EI work together with each person in the team to set the realistic measures that will bring out the very best in their performance and deliverables.

Ask, ask, tell

While EI is very much about understanding those around us and how to bring out the best in each person, it is also about balancing this with who we are and ensuring expectations and respect are present. Most leaders with high EI tend to adopt a coaching style that encourages others to own their performance and find the way to get the required solution, rather than telling them how to do it. This creates trust and empowerment.

On a side note, the old saying, 'You have to earn trust' is well and truly outdated, especially when it comes to adults in the workplace. Trust is something that I hand out on a silver platter to each and every person I meet. Every person has my trust until they give me a reason to no longer trust them. Be open to the possibility rather than limiting.

Back to 'ask, ask, tell': there is a very fine line with this approach, and it is important to know when to draw this line.

Approaching leadership from an 'ask, ask, tell' angle encourages, but also maintains, respect and management at the same time. The way it works is that we use open communication to *ask* someone to do—or how to achieve—something, rather than telling them. 'Are you able to run that report for me please by tomorrow afternoon?'.

If they don't deliver after the first time, we give them the benefit of the doubt and ask again 'Did you get a chance to run that report for me?'. If they still haven't acted after we've asked them twice, there is a high chance that the mind has decided that this isn't a high priority based on the potential gain and potential loss. It has either parked the task or disregarded it.

If we continue to ask, the subconscious mind will realise that there really isn't a consequence for not delivering and it can remain a low priority or be disregarded because they don't stand to lose anything should they not deliver.

Respect is now in question. For many BFF leaders, who like to be liked, this is when the line between being liked and being respected is drawn. That's why, after asking twice, we move to 'tell'. We keep the emotion out of it, and remain calm and purely factual, telling them exactly what needs to be done, and by when, and setting clear expectations, including consequences should the task not be completed. 'I want you to stop what you are doing and focus on running that report. It's required by 2 pm in order to deliver the update to the CEO and is a priority over everything else. If this can't be delivered, let's discuss this now before we go any further.'

This is the ultimate balance of EI in leadership. Without this step, EI can be tainted with the 'fluff' or 'buzz' brush that lets people do what they please.

EI is ultimately about getting the best outcome for everyone while considering each person's emotional driver. If this fine line is missed, it's not the best outcome for anyone.

Feel it

- When we're displaying empathy, we recognise the emotion and severity of the emotion a person is feeling and recall, 'When was the last time I felt that emotion at that severity level?'

- The ultimate purpose of being empathetic is to respond based on the other person's emotional needs and to get the desired outcome rather than escalating the emotion.

- The five-step process for being empathetic and having difficult conversations involves listening and asking open questions; acknowledging and pausing; asking, 'How do we fix this?'; taking action; and giving support.

- Leadership is not a job title, it is a skill. Putting people in leadership roles without leadership training is like putting someone in a technical role without technical training.

- Great leaders have the ability to pause, get out of their own mind and learn to understand the people around them and what makes them tick. A team that is happy and inspired will outperform a team that is led by fear.

- Understanding and appreciating what motivates each person and their real emotional driver is the key to helping them reach their full superstar potential.

- A great leader has the ability to adapt and balance all styles of leadership. They can recognise the needs of the individual and the situation, knowing exactly what style of leadership is needed.

- We all play many roles both inside and outside of work. Understanding the role that we play and the roles that others around us play helps us to understand how to create the perfect, balanced team with team members who complement each other's skills.

- There is a fine line between being liked and being respected as a leader. This is a result of knowing when to 'ask' or coach, and when to 'tell' or manage.

Chapter 8

Ask it: Communicating with influence and purpose

I recall watching a documentary on television with my husband some years ago that referenced the book *The Female Brain* by Louann Brizendine. The program cited that on average women speak 20000 words per day and men only 7000. They made jokes about how by the time a male and female return home from work, the male has likely spoken his 7000 words for the day, while the female still has 13000 left to go. My husband glanced over at me with a look on his face that said it all.

Interestingly, the author of the book later deemed this to be an unreliable study. A further study was done by The University of Texas and The University of Arizona where they recorded nearly 400 university students for up to 10 days between 1984 and 2004. They found that gender didn't play that big of a role in words spoken, with women speaking on average 16215 and men averaging 15669. That amounts to about 15 words every waking minute! The highest recording was a male with 47000 words in one day (nearly one per second) and the lowest recording was also a male with 500 words.

Either way, these studies show that words are our main form of communication and while they have been around for as long as humans have, words are still repeatedly noted as being the main thing that either makes or breaks any form of relationship.

Highly successful organisations usually list communication as playing a key role, while organisations that are struggling or not performing also list communication as playing a key role. This extends to relationships outside of the workplace and in our homes, with forms of communication regularly being listed as the most common reason for divorce and any relationship breakdown. Based on that, we can assume that our ability to communicate effectively, and the words we choose to use, should be a high priority.

Asking creates ownership

No-one likes being told what to do unless it's an emergency or they specifically ask for it. Our mind always likes to have answers, so when we can't extract an answer ourselves, we go looking for it—but asking for an answer is different from being told what to do.

Being told what to do is also like being told we are wrong or have done something at a lower level than expected, or having our ability questioned. Asking questions in this circumstance helps to create ownership. Rather than telling someone that what they did was incorrect, or giving people the answer, asking a question passes the ownership back to them. That way they find their own answer and their mind is more open to accepting it and storing it.

> One of my top performers had hit a slump. I didn't know what was going on, but I'd given him long enough to see whether it was just a few off days. He wasn't performing: he knew it and I knew it. It needed to be addressed. Rather than going in and calling it out to him, I went in and asked him first. 'How are you? Is everything all right? You don't seem yourself lately? I've noticed your results are down.'
>
> Asking a number of questions brings to light the issue but does it in a way that the other person owns the outcome and the response.

> The first answer I received was 'Yeah, I'm okay'. As I continued to ask questions, he went further into his subconscious mind. I could see the truth, ownership and even a reality check hitting him.
>
> We avoided a defensive response and had an honest conversation about how he was lacking motivation and felt like his 'mojo' was gone. This was not the time to tell him how to get it back and what I expected. This was the time to ask him, 'So how are we going to fix this? Where to from here?'
>
> Although I used the 'we' approach, he responded knowing that he had to own it and get himself back on track. We spoke about the coming months, what was coming up and my expectations, and what frame of mind he should be in to nail this and be back to his high-performing self. We created some actions/goals together and I offered my support in any way I could help. Within months he was back to being my highest performer and had an outstanding year!
>
> Asking the right questions creates ownership and a completely different outcome. Maybe if I had gone in there with the approach of *telling* him, rather than *asking* him, that he was underperforming and it wasn't good enough, I might have got the same outcome. There is a high possibility that I also would have got a highly defensive response and created a divide that then brought about a negative mindset.

We don't like being told what to do or that we are in the wrong. A simple flip of approach can create a completely different outcome and mindset. The purpose of communication is the outcome, not the vehicle in which it is delivered. Sometimes we put our pride aside in order to get the right outcome for everyone. Bringing the 'ask, ask, tell' method in from chapter 7 will help to get the right outcome.

Contagious communication

Much like emotions, words and communication are also highly contagious.

Have you ever spent an amount of time overseas and returned home with a bit of an accent? Or did you arrive from another country and have you slowly lost your accent over time?

My dad is from England and his accent is pretty much gone, unless he is speaking to one of his relatives—then out it comes out in all of its glory!

We also create our own vocabulary, with certain 'buzzwords'—such as 'moving forward', 'deep dive', 'big data', 'content is king' and 'journey'—making their way into the workplace. As soon as they start getting traction, we hear them in every meeting, email or conversation. The business world's buzzword for 2020, when COVID-19 hit, was 'pivot'.

Outside of work is no different. Trying to understand what my kids are saying makes me feel old. It's like they are speaking a different language, with words having a completely different meaning from what they previously had.

This shows just how contagious words are. We hear them, we take them into our subconscious mind and they become a part of our communication method, even attaching themselves to our emotions. We tend to use the same descriptive words to describe certain emotions. If we are really angry, we might be furious or fuming. These words tend to rub off on the people around us who, once they've heard them often enough, attach them to their emotions as descriptive words.

Filler words

One of the most frequent words we hear is the one we attach to nerves. This word is often described as a 'filler word'. For example, when we are asked to do something that makes us a little nervous—such as public speaking—all of a sudden, we notice we fill any pause or nervous point with our 'filler word'. For many people it is 'umm'; however, this differs with each person. I know that I say the words 'actually', 'so' and 'absolutely' a lot when I am speaking live. It's like our brain has been wired to insert that word when pressure or nerves become apparent.

Filler words can also be used by people who like to keep control of a conversation. If there is a filler word joining all of our sentences together, then nobody else has the opportunity to interrupt or say anything.

There are a couple of ways of working on reducing these words or rewiring our brain to detach them from that emotion. The first way is awareness. Ever bought a new car and then noticed how many of those cars are everywhere on the road? I know many women who feel like they see other pregnant women everywhere when they are pregnant!

Once our mind is made aware of something specific, we tend to notice it a lot more. I only became aware of my overuse of the word 'absolutely' when I was listening to a radio interview and my kids pointed it out to me. A friend also pointed out to me that I use the word 'actually' a lot. So now that I'm aware of this, I pull myself up on it a split second before either of these words come out of my mouth.

The power of the pause

Another way of reducing words or rewiring your brain to detach them from an emotion is the power of the pause.

I've already referenced the power of the pause several times in the book so it's time to really stop (or dare I say pause) and talk about what this magical gift of communication is.

From the moment we are born, we are encouraged to talk. From our first words through to our last. This makes talking comfortable so it's no wonder that when we hear silence it can become awkward and we naturally fill the silence by talking.

It gives our mind something to focus on, whether we are talking out loud or running through the script in our mind. We have even got to the point where we talk to ourselves.

I do a bit of work from home when I am building new content or prepping for programs. I find that I talk to myself out loud quite often to break the silence and to get my mind processing where I need it to be. I do admit that I have sometimes reached the stage where I am talking to myself, then I make a bit of a joke about what I said and take it one step further to find myself laughing at my own joke. That's definitely the time to get up and take a walk outside.

Pausing is all about stopping. Stopping our flow of communication to give our mind a chance to catch up. It sounds easy, right? But it is going against the natural wiring of our brain. In order to pause, we first give ourselves permission to pause, making it okay to be silent—to be comfortable with the silence. Not only do we need to be comfortable with the silence, but we need the expression on our face to show the people around us that the silence is okay. If there is silence and an extremely worried or nervous look appears on our face, it shows that this silence is not supposed to be happening; whereas if it's a silence accompanied with a comfortable, at ease or purposeful look, then it feels like it belongs.

Once we are comfortable with the pause, it's time to focus on our breathing. We know that deep breaths and oxygen help us to think more clearly. In that moment of pause, take a deep breath in and let your mind think. Once we get past the filler word attached to the emotion, we can access our logical mind. We are quietening the emotion and accessing the information. This is a fantastic tool for when we are talking, presenting or communicating and we forget where we are at, or if we're trying to stop using filler words.

While we are pausing, something magical is happening with the other person/people. The pause first creates confusion in their mind. They are thinking, 'Why is there a pause?' They first look to the emotion that is playing on our face to see if there is permission to pause. If there is, they might start recalling what was the last thing we said ... It must have been important. It might grab their attention back to get them really listening again or, given they are also wired to fill silence with talking, they might start talking to fill the gap.

This becomes a powerful tool for observing what people are really thinking or for getting other people to contribute. The longer we pause, the deeper they will go into their subconscious mind, potentially the more awkward they will feel, and then someone is likely to say something. If we continue to pause, they will add more to what they have already said.

When I run workshops on how to pause, the room is completely aware of what we are learning. I even tell them I'm going to test it out on someone to show how it works and still, every single time, the attendee fills the silence by talking. They don't want to, but they simply can't help themselves.

> One of my first MC opportunities was to host our CEO on his tour to our state. There was a room of around 300 people and prior to the session I asked him which ones out of the pre-submitted questions he wanted me to ask in Q&A time if there weren't any questions.
>
> He told me not to ask any of them — just to wait for a question to come. I replied by asking him, 'What if we don't get any questions?' Again, he told me to just pause and wait for one.
>
> At the event, we got to Q&A time and there was silence. I started to feel really awkward, but he sat there with a smile on his face waiting and I could hear his words in my head, so I waited. After what felt like minutes but was more likely 15 seconds, two hands shot up into the air. While they were asking questions, more hands were raised. After 15 minutes of questions we had to close the session because we ran out of time. This has stuck with me, and pausing is now a standard part of all of my communication.

Allow people time to go into their subconscious mind. Allow yourself time to take a breath and reach your logical mind. Allow time to have a more meaningful and powerful conversation.

The emotional undertone of words

The words we use say a lot about our emotional state and our ability, and they help to create our personal branding. They can be the triggers for other people's emotions the same as other people's words can be our triggers. Our words are also communication from our subconscious mind that tells us how we are feeling about what we are saying or doing.

Say the following sentences out loud and listen to the impact of each one because of the undertone of the word that has been changed:

- I have to go to the shops.

- I need to go to the shops.

- I can't go to the shops.

- I want to go to the shops.

- I will go to the shops.

- I am going to the shops.

Each of these words carries a different emotional undertone and communicates to our subconscious mind how motivated we are to really do it. This same undertone carries through in the communications we use in the workplace.

If I arrive at work and say to myself, 'I have to do this report' or 'I need to do this report', chances are I don't really want to do it and my subconscious mind will provide me with many different ways to distract myself from actually doing the report.

However, if I were to say, 'I am doing this report', the decision has been made and my subconscious mind knows that's exactly what I'm doing and will support me to do it.

Our mind likes to be right and therefore our subconscious mind will do whatever is required to match the emotional decision that we have already made through the words we choose.

The emotional undertone of our words not only impacts our subconscious mind and our ability to deliver, it also impacts those around us and the effectiveness of the communication.

Here are some handpicked words that are currently misused, overused or have the greatest emotional undertone impact on us and those around us.

'Sorry'

The word 'sorry' has become such a common word used in so many circumstances. Let me clarify that 'sorry' is a word that absolutely should be used. If we do something wrong or there is a reason to apologise, then say sorry! Never be above saying sorry. Owning our errors or mistakes is step 1 in EI. It is the core of self-awareness. We can also be sorry for someone else through sympathy and empathy. Sorry is a word, like many, that creates a level of stature. When we are sorry, the word naturally lifts the other person's stature higher than ours. So, when we use the word 'sorry', know that the emotional undertone is creating that stature.

There is a fantastic short video online showing the impact of the emotional undertone of the word 'sorry'. It is an old Pantene ad from 2014 that captures several women throughout the day starting sentences with the word sorry. One lady knocks on an office door saying, 'Sorry, have you got a minute?' Another lady, who is in a meeting, says, 'Sorry, I have a silly question.' A lady using a common armrest between two seats when a man sits in the seat beside her removes her arm, saying 'sorry'. In every situation throughout the ad, the word is used less as an apology and more out of habit and lack of confidence or worthiness.

This is not about stopping using the word 'sorry'. This is about understanding the stature that is created due to the emotional undertone of the word. Have a think about how and when you use the word 'sorry'.

Do you use the word 'sorry' in the right context? Is it creating the right stature?

The Pantene ad shows that in a majority of circumstances, we can drop the word 'sorry' and the sentence will still make sense. The emotional undertone (and power) of the sentence completely changes.

'Busy'

'Busy' has become like an epidemic. It is used to describe how we feel, though it certainly isn't an emotion. We find ourselves using it in response to a greeting. It seems as though if we aren't busy today, then we can't really be succeeding. Then the competitive side comes out: 'You think *you're* busy, you should see how busy *I* am!' It has become such common language and practice for us all to be overloaded and always in a rush. Let's remove ourselves from the 'busy' situation for a moment and really look at the emotional undertone that this epidemic is causing.

If you contacted me to ask a question or to have a chat and started by asking how I was only for me to respond with 'busy', how would you feel?

When you are looking to have a conversation with someone and you ask them how are they feeling and they say 'busy', what is the emotional impact on you?

For most of us, it either creates a blocker to the conversation or it can make us feel guilty that we are taking up their valuable time.

That whatever we want to say had better be important because they are so busy. Again, it creates an instant stature between the people communicating. Our natural defence to match that stature is to say that we are also very busy. If we aren't looking to match that stature, then we might wrap up the conversation pretty quickly.

Being constantly busy, or on the go, also has us living a large part of our time in our conscious mind, as though in autopilot. We know our mind needs a break. We also know our subconscious mind is reportedly 30000 times more powerful than our conscious mind so we really aren't performing at our best. Being busy for long periods of time can also lead to overwhelm. We will talk more about managing our 'busy' in chapter 9.

Unlike the word 'sorry', I encourage you to reduce your use of the word 'busy'. Call yourself out on it. If someone asks you how you are, they are asking how you are feeling emotionally. Tap into your subconscious mind and tell them about what's been happening and how you are really feeling. This can go a long way to harbouring an effective conversation and building a genuine relationship.

'Just'

'Just wanted to check ...'

How often do you start an email or any communication with the word 'just'?

The word 'just' is similar to 'sorry' and we can throw in 'busy' as well. 'Sorry, just checking how that request is coming along. I know you're busy.' The word 'just' creates instant stature, the same as the other two words.

> To understand the stature created by any word,
> think about how it makes you feel about the
> other person when it is said to you.

I received a phone call earlier this year from a young lady in the media industry. As soon as I answered my phone, straight after introducing herself she said, 'Sorry to interrupt you, Amy. I know you are very busy. I just wondered if you have enough time to answer a few questions for an article?'

I stopped her right there and let her know that I chose to answer my phone and of course I have the time to speak with her. My time is no more valuable than her time. She gave out a sigh of relief as she explained she had been yelled at several times that morning for interrupting people.

Don't ever be that person. Understand the impact our words have on other people. The emotional undertone can completely change their day and even their beliefs.

'Try'

When we try, we attempt to make something happen. If we use the word 'try' before we make the attempt, we have already sent a message to our subconscious mind that it's unlikely we will succeed but, hey, we will give it a go.

This instantly diminishes our chances, remembering again that our mind likes to be right so if we have sent a message to our subconscious mind that we will 'try', our subconscious mind is going to do everything it can to make the emotional undertone of the word come true: 'It's very unlikely but, hey, let's humour them and give it a try.'

If you asked me to complete an important task for you and I answered it with 'I'll try', how confident would you be that I will deliver?

'Impossible'

Nothing is impossible. The same as there is always time and a way to do something. It simply comes down to how badly we want it and what we are willing to do for it to happen.

Using the word 'impossible' closes our mind down to any options or ways to make it happen. We have effectively written it off. If someone tries to give us a solution, our conscious mind might go into defence mode and provide every reason possible why that solution won't work. Our mind is always looking for the quickest and easiest solution and if that can't be done, then at times we default to it being impossible.

I was managing a large team and we received a complaint from one of our customers. The customer had already raised the issue with three other people and hadn't received a resolution. Their situation was a bit unique in that they needed our claims team to follow a slightly different claims process for their group of customers.

I asked to meet with all of the internal stakeholders to better understand the situation. The claims person told me that it wasn't possible to follow the requested process because the system physically wouldn't allow it. The IT person agreed with them and said there wasn't an option within the system to do this or to change it without spending years and millions of dollars to upgrade the system. The admin person agreed with them and the technical expert said it didn't faze them and had no bearing on the technical assessment. The consensus in the room was that it was impossible and that's what they had told the customer.

At that point, I sat back and paused. Then I said to them, 'Let's assume this complaint goes all the way to the CEO and he tells us it has to happen, no matter what. What would we do then?' Again, I paused for a long period of time.

First, the claims person said, 'I guess I could process it manually. I mean it will take about three times as long to do and I might need to get an extra staff member in to help.'

Then the admin person said, 'We could get it all into an Excel spreadsheet and help with the extra admin steps needed due to the manual process.'

The IT person spoke up and said, 'Actually, I could run a file export that we could then export into Excel.' I sat back and listened as they worked together to come up with a process. Yes it was manual, but it was happening. 'So, it is possible?' I asked.

The claims person said, 'Well yes, it's going to take a lot more time and effort, but we can make it work.' My response: 'Fantastic, let's do it!'

It certainly wasn't the easiest or the quickest way. It took disrupting their mindsets and removing choice to make it something that had to happen, but we got the right outcome in the end.

There are many real-life stories and movies that document people who decide when they are young children that they are going to one day compete at the Olympics. They don't know in what sport—and they don't really care either. They just know that they are going to the Olympics and from there, they make it happen.

Nothing is impossible; it comes down to our priorities. How badly we want it and what we are willing to do.

'Fail'

The word 'fail' carries an emotional undertone that many of us struggle to embrace, or to want to embrace. Failure is defined as 'an absence or lack of success'.

Given we are programmed from a young age to be successful and to have the right answer, the emotional undertone of 'fail' goes against everything our brain tells us should happen.

We know that in every situation there is an opportunity to learn and grow, even if we are learning what not to do. If 'fail' is still a word you struggle to align to, try changing the word or the trigger to achieve the same outcome: learning and growth.

I don't fail. For me, a lack of success would mean that there was no growth or learning that I could take away and that I had simply given up. This never happens because I can always recognise some type of learning or growth opportunity that leads me to reflect, implement and continue to move forward.

How we define 'fail' impacts the ultimate outcome.

Communication is about the recipient, not us

One of the biggest misconceptions with communication is that we think it is about us. We communicate in a way that works for us rather than realising communication is completely about the recipient of the message. If the recipient doesn't receive the communication correctly, then the communication hasn't been successful.

With that in mind, we should be communicating our messages the way we know the recipient needs to receive them. This not only includes the communication method that we choose but also the language. If we try to communicate to someone in English who only speaks Chinese, then the communication is not going to be successful. All diversity aspects should come into the equation, along with the preferred method. If we are ever unsure of what is required, test it out.

My son, Koen, asked what was for dinner a while back. I told him we were having quiche. He turned up his nose and said: 'Really? I don't like quiche. Can't we have something different?' I responded (tongue in cheek) with, 'Hmmm, what about bacon and egg pie?' 'Yum, yes please, Mum!'

A simple change of communication language and the outcome was completely different. I didn't lie to him as my version of quiche is bacon and egg pie. It's not like I changed the name or the recipe or served him something completely different. What I did was adapt to his language and communication. He didn't know what quiche was and his subconscious mind had helped him to decide that he didn't like the sound of this unknown food. He was familiar with bacon and egg and could align dinner to his memory — which is stored in the subconscious mind — which told him how much he likes those two foods.

I could have said, 'Tough luck, that's what's for dinner!' I could have sat down at the table with him and made him eat every mouthful of the food that his mind had pre-decided he definitely didn't like. Instead, we had an enjoyable dinner and he inhaled his food, loving it. He was smart enough to ask me after dinner whether they are the same thing and I told him they sure are. It was a good lesson for him on not judging something based simply on a name or on his lack of knowledge or experience.

Like many elements of EI, at times we put our pride aside to see something from the other person's point of view as well as our own. It becomes about getting the desired outcome. I didn't cook a different meal. I didn't make any change to what I was doing other than change my language, which completely changed the experience and the outcome. I didn't have to convince or battle with him to eat it and he enjoyed eating it. Dinner was a whole lot easier and more pleasant.

Our ability to see and deliver communication from both sides rather than just from our own has a direct impact on our personal brand. While this example showed it from a family point of view, we frequently see opportunities like this in the workforce. How we handle each communication situation will help to form other people's opinions and perceptions of us.

We know that perceptions are really reality. Someone's perception of us, whether we agree with it or not, is their reality until they decide to change that perception. We hear a lot that what people say about us when we are not in the room is our personal brand. I would take it one step further and say that how we talk and what we say about other people who aren't in the room says more about us than anything else.

Meetings with purpose

When we walk into a room, the seat we choose to sit on says a lot about us and sets an emotional tone. Before we talk about the right seat to choose, we should have a clear understanding of why we are walking in the room in the first place and the role we are about to play. Whether it is a meeting or an event, everything we do should have a purpose. Sitting in the room simply to keep the seat warm is a complete waste of time for us and for everyone else in the room.

Here are five questions to ask ourselves before committing to any meeting, conversation or event:

1. *What is the purpose and proposed outcome of this meeting?*
   What do I want to walk away with? What do I want others to walk away with?

2. *What is the emotional need I am fulfilling for the attendees or for myself?*
   Everything we do is for an emotional driver or outcome.
   How will I feel if this meeting serves its purpose? How will others feel?

3. *Is there an agenda?*
   What will happen in the meeting? How will it run? What will we cover? Where do we start? How long will it go for?

4. *Are the right people invited?*
   Do we have everyone we need in the room to achieve the desired purpose and outcome? Is there anyone in the room who is not required? Too many people in the room can result in distractions and less emotional connection when trying to get the right outcome.

5. *Is a meeting the best form of communication?*
   Why do we need to be here right now, together? Could this be done via email? What is the purpose of human connection?

Team meetings are a perfect example of the purpose of human connection. Team meetings are rarely about the information as information can easily be provided by email. We hold team meetings to create a connection, a bond, an opportunity to communicate with the other team members to create relationships. When team meetings turn into information dumps, they have lost their core purpose.

Once we are confident that the meeting has purpose and everything else required to achieve the desired outcome, we then need to understand the role we are to play in the meeting. Why were we invited? What value will we bring to this meeting?

Figure 3 outlines the four key roles played in meetings.

Chairperson

The role of the chairperson is to ensure the meeting achieves exactly what it set out to achieve. They are effectively running the meeting in alignment with the agenda. The chairperson can be a facilitator who doesn't need to know anything about the specifics of the meeting other than the purpose, timing and agenda. They could also be the expert in the room.

Quite often the person with expertise on the subject matter of the meeting takes the role of chairperson. If the meeting includes a team of some type, the leader may generally chair the meeting. Rotating the chairperson provides growth and opportunity for others. It also mixes up the process and creates change, which is when our conscious mind can get confused and draw in our subconscious mind for assistance. This can create more focus and opportunity for the emotional mind to be involved.

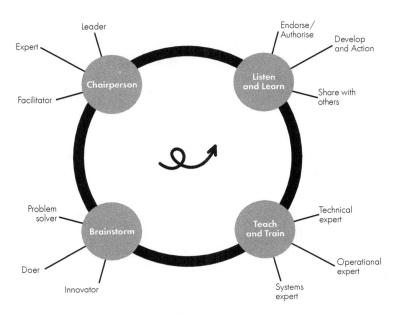

Figure 3: roles played in meetings

Listen and learn

Your role may be to listen and learn. Sometimes we are invited to a meeting to receive information and learn from it. It doesn't have to be a training session; we might be invited because the information that is being discussed is something we should be aware of. We might be the person who needs to endorse or authorise the information or there might be a need to develop actions on the other side. We can even be there representing a number of people and taking in the information, ready to share it with others after the meeting.

Regardless of the reason, if the role we are playing is to listen and learn, we should arrive with a notebook and show that the purpose has been achieved through body language or confirmation. Going to any meeting or event without taking notes sends an emotional undertone that we don't deem anything about the meeting as being important enough to note down.

Brainstorm

We may have been invited to the meeting to brainstorm. Three types of people make up the brainstorming role in meetings, as shown in figure 3.

Are we the innovator, who challenges the way others are thinking or doing things? Or the problem solver, who complements the innovator, bringing the best of ideas together and solving any obstacles or blockages along the way? Or perhaps we are the doer: the person who combines the results from the innovator and problem solver and turns them into measurable actions to ensure they actually happen.

Entering a meeting playing the role of a brainstormer means that our mindset should be in an open and creative position, which definitely requires tapping into the subconscious mind.

Teach and train

Are we the teacher or the trainer of the meeting? Maybe we are there to deliver information to the other people in the meeting.

Even when we are teaching or training, it's important to remember what expertise we are bringing to the table and to stay in our own lane. Are we the systems expert, the operational expert or the technical expert? What is our expertise and what do people want to hear from us?

* * *

It is very possible that we might play several roles in one meeting or even find ourselves moving into other roles during the meeting. Either way, if we are not clear on the role we are playing, ask the organiser prior to the meeting. Being at a meeting without a specific role makes us a seat warmer. Our mind will check out and it becomes wasted time.

Choosing the right seat

Now that we have purpose and understand the role we are playing in the meeting, let's pick the right seat to have the greatest impact on the outcome.

Head of the table

This is the perfect place to sit to have access to all people in the room and to create natural lead and control. It's often used by the chairperson or organiser of the meeting. It's also a great place to sit if we are the trainer or teacher. If we are looking to blend into the meeting and not draw attention to ourselves, then this is definitely not the place to sit.

Middle seat

The middle seat, surrounded by everyone, creates a togetherness. It helps to create an even stature and is really effective in brainstorming sessions. The middle seat also tends to be in the perfect peripheral position for whoever is at the head of the table.

If we really want to make an impact, or be noticed by someone specific in the meeting, a middle seat that is at either end of their peripheral vision will be an advantage. Smiling, being engaged and acknowledging what is being said also helps.

Conflict in the room

If there is anyone in the room we generally or potentially could have conflict with, our natural default is to sit opposite them. This instantly creates an 'us and them' subconscious feeling and may trigger or increase the chance of conflict. Sitting right next to the person creates an equal stature and we tend to challenge or ask questions the least with those sitting next to us.

* * *

Our emotional intelligence in a meeting, or with any group of people, begins with the role we are playing and the seat we sit in. Our subconscious mind is always working in the background. Understand what emotional undertone is being sent to the people around you and what emotional outcome you will walk away with.

Practising EI in meetings

Regardless of how well we have prepared, our behaviour during a meeting is what leaves the lasting impression. Here are a few things to avoid, with some definitely being career-limiting moves:

- playing on your phone, being distracted, having your own conversation or not paying attention

- bad body language, slouching, arms folded, defensive stance

- leaving the room randomly without a reason or it being pre-organised

- speaking over other people or constantly being negative

- leaving your video off in a video conference

- arriving late or not arriving at all

- delegating without advising the organiser prior to the meeting

- turning up without a notepad/device

- heckling, judging or making derogative jokes.

What is your commitment and how present are you in meetings?

How many things do we do that we really aren't 100 per cent committed to? If we aren't committed to something, why do it?

I was working with some amazing men who run a very elite program for middle-aged men who have lost their identity or are generally struggling with everything. The commitment level is high, as it should be when we decide to change our life for the better.

One of their commitments was that you turn up on time every time, you deliver exactly what has been asked of you and you are present. The first time I met with the director and one of his board, the director had a mix-up of times due to us being in different time zones and was two minutes late to dial in to the meeting.

This is where I learned the consequence for him was 500 burpees done with a 10 kg weight vest on. Why? Standards. That simple. The punishment had to be done within 24 hours, recorded on time lapse and shared with the attendees of the meeting. The purpose behind this was to ensure everyone was 100 per cent committed to the program, turned up on time and was present and focused on everything they did.

> The third time I met with them, I was one minute late to dial in to the meeting. They laughed and laughed. They said the consequence was 200 burpees in a 24-hour period, but I knew they wouldn't hold me to it! Nevertheless, I held myself to it. If it was good enough for them to turn up on time committed and present at our meetings then they deserved that level of respect back.
>
> For someone who rarely exercised at that time, and certainly couldn't do 200 burpees straight, I changed my mindset and managed to do those 200 burpees, 10 at a time, throughout the day — and delivered my time lapse video to them. Other than struggling to walk, and even breathe, for the next two days, I learned something really big from it.

Getting that commitment right in our mindset and giving it our wholehearted attention is turning up as the best version of ourselves.

How many meetings, catch-ups, events, even phone calls do you show up to as the best version of yourself?

When a meeting comes to an end, revisit the original purpose to ensure it was achieved and review the actions or next steps. It's always good to check that the meeting was effective and that the ultimate emotional outcome was achieved.

EI and emails

In February 2020, data from The Radicati Group detailed that we were exceeding 306 billion emails worldwide sent every day. They predicted that this would be at around 361 billion by 2024. This was prior to the real impact of the COVID-19 pandemic, which showed an even greater increase of emails as face-to-face communication became restricted.

The pandemic created flexibility in the working environment, with more people working from home and extended working hours. This resulted in fewer people communicating face to face and it became likely that the number of emails would continue to increase more quickly than originally expected.

As email swiftly becomes the number one preferred method of communication, it challenges everything we have ever known about effective communication.

We have always known that body language and tone can be far more important than the actual message and when we are dealing with emails, these are both absent. So, when someone reads an email, their subconscious mind—based on the current environment, their emotions, the preconception of the sender and/or the topic—creates the tone and body language that it perceives goes with the email.

We know how dangerous that can be! Especially when we are pumping out emails as fast as our fingers can type them. It's no wonder communication becomes diluted, inaccurate or misinterpreted.

Given the limitations that email creates to the effectiveness of communication, it is absolutely essential to leverage EI within our emails.

Emails leave a permanent trail and mark on our brand. Before we get into how to include EI in our emails, let's talk about things to avoid when considering sending an email.

CC'ing and BCC'ing

Carbon copying (CC'ing) is a great tool for creating efficiencies if a copy of an email needs to form part of a file or if a group of people are working on something together and they all need to be kept updated, or even for introducing someone. It effectively saves us from a second email right then and there.

Unfortunately, the CC tool has become overused by many people, contributing greatly to why we feel so 'busy'. It has become the new normal to copy a handful of people into each email and create a back-and-forth email trail because we think everyone needs to know everything that is happening at all times. The information becomes overwhelming and there is no way to store all this information in our mind.

I work with a lot of leaders who spend the majority of their day either emailing or in meetings and it's impacting their productivity and mindset. It's interesting to see that most of them ask their staff to copy them into emails that they 'need to know about'. CC'ing can be a form of micromanagement and decreases empowerment in individuals to take control of situations and be comfortable to ask for help only when needed.

If something arises and the leader needs to get involved, they are not likely to rely on remembering an email they read two weeks ago. There is a good chance they won't even rely on searching for the email and reading it. They are likely to go straight to the person involved and ask them for full details on it or they will go to the file to read the background. The email trail that they have been copied into over the past month is likely to be confusing and a waste of their time and mind capacity.

If we look at the number of times we are copied into, or copy others into, emails and spend time and capacity reading them (or even clearing them) compared to how many actually escalate, it doesn't justify the 'what if' of something occurring that requires the involvement of a leader.

Imagine for a moment that you didn't receive all the emails you're CC'd into. Would that make a difference to your day? If the answer is yes, then review the process.

We do not need to know everything that happens every moment of the day. Rewire your brain to trust and empower those around you.

CC'ing others into emails can be used as a scare tactic to make recipients take action when they see who is copied in. I can see the logic in this, and I know it can work, but what it also does is kill the credibility of the person sending the email. It is telling the person we copied in, and the recipient, that 'I haven't got a hold of this situation and I need your name and stature to help me'. It will cause damage to the relationship between the person sending the email and the recipient of the email because it's like 'dobbing' and it decreases the credibility and respect of the sender in the eyes of the person who has been CC'd into the email.

There is only one good reason I have come across to use BCC (blind carbon copy). This is when an email is going to several people and we can't disclose their email addresses as part of privacy.

If I send an email to all of my subscribers, all email addresses should be BCC'd to maintain privacy. When BCC is used in confrontational or workplace emails, it has been compared to the electronic version of gossiping. Why would we need someone to read an email but not want anyone to know that they have read the email? I'm yet to find an emotionally intelligent reason to do this.

Inferior or aggressive words

An email is no place for intimidating or aggressive words. If there is a tough message to deliver, it should always be done face to face where possible, even if that's over a video call. In such instances, emails should be an absolute last resort and even then, they can probably wait until the message can be communicated face to face.

We can take it one step further to say that an email should never be sent when we are in a highly emotional state. It is way too easy to smash out our emotions in an email or on an electronic platform. Remember that anything electronic provides a permanent trail and mark. When the communication is read it won't just include evidence of your highly emotional state, it will also affect the recipient's emotional reaction. This absolutely lacks EI. I highly recommend sleeping on it before deciding if an email really should be sent.

No novels

Based on our modalities, we can be either highly detailed people or only want the high-level details. Communication is all about the recipient, so sending a long, detailed, novel-like email to a big-picture, high-level kind of person means there is a good chance they are going to open it, see the length, then close it straight away without even reading it. If the email requires a lot of information, maybe a phone call with a follow-up summary email is more appropriate? Or an attachment to the email; or at the very least headings within the email and a high-level summary at the top.

In contrast, if the recipient is a very detail-oriented person, they will want the full details or they are likely to send an email back with questions requesting more information. We should know who we are sending the email to before writing it and remember it is about them, not us.

Poor timing

Timing can be a concern when it comes to sending and receiving emails. Is it appropriate to send a work email out of hours, late at night, in the early hours of the morning or even on weekends? With the availability of smart devices, switching off from work continues to become more of a challenge. This is where ownership comes into play.

If you are the person sending the email outside of working hours, is there a reason for it? Flexible working hours allow for a variety of working arrangements to better suit many people. As long as the sender is getting the right balance between work and play, that's what matters.

If you are the person receiving the email and are feeling like you need to respond, you need to own your actions. If we don't want to open the email, then we simply don't. If we don't even want to know it's there, we can switch off our email notifications. Own the decision—no-one is standing beside us forcing us to look at it, read it or respond to it. We have the ability to make our own decision based on our priorities and consequences at the time. Only we can decide this. Own it.

Influencing in emails

Much like meetings and anything we do in life, every email should have a clear purpose and expected outcome. What do we want the response to be? Do we want a response? What kind of response would be ideal? It's important to have answers to these questions before we even draft the email. We should also use these questions as a checklist before sending an email.

The process outlined in figure 4 brings EI into the words we use in emails and leverages the process our mind goes through to help us achieve the desired outcome.

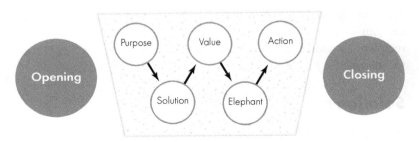

Figure 4: influencing through email

Opening

In the opening line, we set the scene. This is the opportunity to create a connection and to help get the recipient into their subconscious mind. It's great if it can stop them in their tracks from flicking through emails in their conscious mind and refocus on our email.

It should always start with a greeting. This greeting should match your own personality and relationship with the recipient. It shouldn't be too different from the way you would talk if you called them or saw them on the street.

Never underestimate the value of the first word. For me, an email that starts with 'Amy', rather than a 'Hi', 'Hello' or Hey', instantly gets on my nerves. I'm a people person so I want to say 'hey' before we get down to business. We do business with people, not products, so the more we can create connection as a person the better.

I'll also ask a question relating to how they are doing or how their week/ weekend has been. Given that asking someone how their weekend has been or how they are doing has become a bit autopilot and lacking in meaning, I show them I mean it by letting them know how I am and what I've been doing. It is me letting them into my life and showing the personal side of myself.

This creates a pause in their thoughts, sending them into their subconscious mind. Sharing a bit about me encourages many to share something with me in return. This is how we build genuine relationships—by caring.

Purpose

We want to make it really obvious upfront what the purpose of the email is. Don't try to hide the email under something else. Our recipient shouldn't have to go looking for a hidden message or reason for the email.

Solution

Emails are usually sent because there is a problem or something that requires information, or an answer. Once the purpose is clear, we should detail the proposed solution. This should align to our purpose and what we are looking to get out of the email.

Value

It's time to call out the value that your solution brings to the situation or the 'what's in it for them'. Let's not kid ourselves, given everything we do is for an emotional outcome, everything we do needs to have something in it for 'me'. Spell out that value and spell out the value for everyone involved.

The elephant in the room

There is always an elephant in the room. The 'elephant' is the obvious response that might come to mind as to why what we are suggesting is not going to work. Assume that your recipient doesn't agree with the purpose, solution or value and calls it out as a potential concern. What would that concern be? Then call out that concern, and explain how you've thought about it and how it can be rectified. This is giving reassurance to the uncertainty in their mind.

Action

What do we want them to do now that they have read our email? Keep it really simple: either list or summarise exactly what the next steps are. The easier this is, the more likely they are to agree. Remember our mind likes to find the easiest and quickest solution. Aim for the action to be a simple 'yes' or 'thanks'.

Be sure to list the alternatives to minimise email trails. 'If your answer is A, then we will require x, y and z; whereas if your answer is B, then we will require q, r and s.' Asking them whether their answer is A or B without letting them know the outcome is guaranteed to produce an email trail. Be transparent and deliver the full picture upfront.

Closing

The closing is just as important as the opening. This is when business is put aside and we loop around the human element and the connection.

The closing is how we maintain and grow relationships, regardless of what business is required in-between. We close an email similarly to how we close a phone call or a face-to-face conversation.

The wording we use in this closing also sets expectations of when we expect to receive a response. If we were to say, 'Enjoy the rest of your week' it shows that at this point, we may not be expecting to communicate with them again this week. Whereas 'Enjoy the rest of your day' implies we are expecting to communicate with them again tomorrow. The time frame we use in this closing will speak to the recipient's subconscious mind, telling it by when they should respond, as well as their relationship and emotional outcomes.

* * *

The words used throughout an email, and in any conversation, should have the appropriate emotional undertone. Communication using the words 'you', 'your' and 'I' can come across as aggressive and create conflict. Whereas the words 'we', 'our' and 'us' create a feeling of partnership, equal stature and togetherness.

Check back on your purpose and expected outcome. Does your email align? Will it likely achieve the expected outcome?

Before sending the email, we should always read it aloud. I don't mean read it in our head. When we read in our head, our mind can insert or change words to match what we are trying to say so errors can be easily missed. We should read it aloud (even if in a whisper voice), forcing our mind to read every single word.

Figure 5 shows an example of an email created using the above process. The email was sent to a high-detail person, hence the length and level of detail within the email. This process can still easily be covered in an email with only four sentences, with each sentence ticking a number of steps.

	Hey Jayde
Opening	Hope <u>you</u> are enjoying the EI Communication Program as much as I am enjoying delivering it. What an awesome group of people <u>we</u> have this round!
Purpose	It's been great testing out the content and timings as we run through the first ever delivery of the 6-week program. I've noticed the first 2 sessions have run longer than 1 hour with both going for 1 hour and 15 mins. This is 15 mins longer than we had anticipated and even then some of the activities seem rushed towards the end.
Solution	I've reviewed the format for the March program and have opted to change to a 3-week program with 2 hours per week instead of 1 hour over 6 weeks.
Value	This reduces the intro, recap and closing for the 6 sessions to 3, allowing more time for content. It also means attendees only need to be available for 3 dates rather than 6.
Elephant	I was concerned that a 2-hour block on a weeknight after spending all day at work might be too much; however, feedback has been that the hour goes really fast and the 3-week commitment is more conducive.
Action	March program dates have just been released for the next round of the Communication Program and the new People Skills/Leadership Program. They are both based on the new structure, being 3 weeks with 2 hours each week. I'd love to hear your thoughts on the new program structures.
Closing	Thank you so much, Jayde, for being a part of the first round of the EI Communication Program. It's always fantastic to have such passionate and honest people in the room while we are refining the timings and content.
	If at any time you need to leave prior to the session finishing, please do so and I am happy to contact you at a later time to run through anything missed.
	Have a fantastic weekend!
	Thanks
	Amy

Figure 5: example of an influential email

Passionate vs egotistical

When tapping into our EI and spending a great deal of time in our subconscious mind, we can become quite passionate about what we do and how we do it. Following The EI Rewiring Process to disrupt our mindset through 'Face it' and 'Feel it' should always help with self-regulation and understanding others, but there are times when we can get caught up in a conversation and our passion becomes egotistical.

I've heard some people justify their lack of EI as being due to their passion about what they do. The line is fine, but there is definitely a difference and learning to identify the point at which we cross the line is about asking ourselves when the focus shifts from being about 'others' to being about 'me'.

Ego is something we all have; ego is not a bad word. It is defined as our level of self-esteem or self-importance. This measure exists in all of us. It is when we cross the line to become egotistical that we refer to it as having a 'big ego'. The word 'egotistical' is described as being excessively conceited or absorbed in ourselves—self-centred, selfish, ego-centric, and the list goes on.

Passion is about having a strong emotion that might be hard to contain or control. Our passion usually aligns heavily to our beliefs and values. Given this, it should be no surprise that everyone's passions differ and people are not always going to agree with one another because their beliefs and values may differ.

When we get really passionate about something, we tend to go into an emotional hijack where our emotions are driving our mind and our logical mind gets parked in the meantime.

Both passion and egotism are strong emotional beliefs. Egotism puts us first, whereas passion wants to share that belief and enthusiasm with others. Core emotions aligned with passion tend to be excitement or love, whereas egotism is conceited and about having to be right. There is a deep focus on 'me' and recognition of our ability or our knowledge with egotism, whereas the deep focus tends to be 'others' and sharing the emotion when we are passionate.

We can all recall someone in our lives who we would describe as passionate as opposed to egotistical. The impacts of each strong emotional belief are extensive, not only on our personal brand but also on how we make others feel. Research shows that the human race benefits greatly from celebrating wins and success, but when is it okay and when does it go too far?

In one workshop I ran, I asked the attendees to tell me something they were really passionate about. One of the ladies raised her hand and said 'baking'!

I continued to ask her questions to really find something specific that she liked to bake, and it turned out it was cookies. I could see the passion all over her face as I asked her to describe her cookies to me.

We were all caught up in her passion as she told us how chocolate chip was one of her favourites and that they are nice, big cookies with that soft fudgy centre. And they're even better when they're eaten straight out of the oven.

There were people in the room who had tried her cookies and agreed that they were amazing. There was no doubt that at that point in time she was extremely passionate about her belief in her ability to make delicious cookies and she wanted everyone to feel that passion and enjoy it too.

I deliberately lost all expression in my face, turned my excitement to a frown and told her that I didn't like soft cookies — that I much preferred crunchy cookies and I wasn't sure I would like her cookies at all. At that point, her posture and emotions changed. She started to tell me why soft cookies are better than crunchy cookies and we went back and forth until she decided that clearly I hadn't tried her cookies and that they were the best, pretty much shutting down the conversation.

This lady was a lovely, highly respected member of the team and would never have been described as egotistical. But at this point, the passion was gone and the line to egotism had been crossed.

Why did this happen?

This all comes back to our minds needing to be right. The natural response is to defend. We come up with every reason why we are right because if the other person is right, that might make us wrong. Being wrong doesn't naturally sit well with us. We saw the point where baking cookies changed from being her passion and sharing it with others to her need to be right, driving her ego higher.

The lady in this story is definitely known as *not* being egotistical. She really is the sweetest person. When she first put up her hand, I wondered how well this example would work given her personality. The truth is, it happens to all of us, so how do we become aware and leverage our EI to limit this from happening?

Let's rewind to when I first told her that I didn't like soft cookies and that I much preferred crunchy cookies. At this point, we ask ourselves, is this conversation or situation right now about me or about others? If it is about others, we should start asking questions in return rather than going into defensive, judgement mode. 'Hmm, how interesting. Amy, tell me why you like crunchy cookies so much?' 'What is it about them that makes them so good?'

There is a reason why people generally don't talk about religion, politics, and even these days, vaccinations and nutritional preferences. They are conversations driven on high levels of belief and can very quickly become an egotistical battle rather than a conversation about passion.

Every single one of us is different and that's what makes us special. Don't 'agree to disagree'. This is a cop-out and is stubborn, sending the message that 'I'm right and you are wrong and I'm sick of trying to convince you of that so I give up.'

Be open to everyone being different and take the time to appreciate it.

Listen, understand, empathise and get to know who they are. That's what makes us so fascinating. Taking in that information might just help us to test out a belief or value and maybe, it might even change one. We do this through asking questions, not forcing opinions and beliefs.

Ask it

- Communication is not about us, it is all about the recipient. It's about their style, needs and ability to understand in order to get the right outcome.

- Great communication means we put our pride aside at times and let the other person find and own the answer.

- Most people don't like being told what to do. Asking questions creates ownership in the other person because they provide the answer.

- Some of the most effective communication methods involve pausing and listening. This is how we really learn about others and what they have to say.

- Every word carries an emotional undertone that creates stature, communicates with the subconscious mind and influences the outcome.

- Communication should always have a clear purpose, whether it is through a verbal conversation, an email or a meeting. We should also know exactly what role we play in the communication.

- Communicating through technology requires high levels of EI to ensure the message, tone and body language are interpreted accurately.

- The fine line between passion and egotism comes down to the ability to ask questions and introduce EI rather than getting defensive.

Chapter 9

Drive it: Being motivated and reaching our full potential

There is very little doubt that humans have some fantastic ideas! Our mind can go into overdrive thinking of all the possible 'what if' moments: 'What if we did it this way instead?' 'What if we redesigned the product to make it better?' 'What if we renovated the house?' The actual ideas are not generally where the problem lies. Moving them from ideas to the implementation stage—now that's a completely different story.

We tend to set out with the very best of intentions only to find 'blockers' in our way. Not enough time, not enough money, not enough energy—it's all too hard and overwhelming. While fear, self-doubt and procrastination can get in the way of many great ideas, the make-up of our brain and our human behavioural needs and responses also play a big role in this process.

Rewiring our brain to achieve targets

There is still much confusion around research on whether our brain can determine the difference between imagination and reality. While some researchers believe the subconscious mind cannot identify the difference between imagination and reality, others say the brain processes the two different areas in completely different ways.

We know that the subconscious mind holds our emotional response, along with our long-term memory, and we know that everything we do is for an emotional outcome or driver. We can picture how we will feel based on each outcome thanks to our memory, values, beliefs and triggers, so whether what we imagine does in fact become reality or simply taps into those memories, values, beliefs and triggers is not completely known.

What I do know is that sometimes I wake up in the morning and the dream I've had during the night seems so real that I struggle to let go of it. I know that I've heard the stories that my husband and his mates tell of their high-school years so many times that I feel like I was there—I can picture and re-tell every one of them! And when my mum pulls out old photos from when I was a baby, I have no idea if it is memories I am recalling or memories of my imagination, which have been created by visualising them each time Mum tells me the stories behind the photos.

If everything we do is for an emotional outcome, the moment we can visually create the image of the end result and attach an emotional outcome to that end result we've embedded that thought in our mind regardless of whether it is imagination or reality. It has emotions attached to it and we know how we would feel if we achieved the desired emotional outcome that we have just visually created. Now that it is embedded in our mind, it makes us want it even more so we can feel that emotional outcome. This gives us a feeling of loss because we know what we could have but currently don't have.

The difference between what we actually have right now and our amazing ideas or goals can be quite extensive, so we may feel overwhelmed thinking how we can possibly get there. Or we may think we'll never have the time or money to make it happen.

With each new idea or goal, we are triggering a chemical in our mind. The key chemical when it comes to motivation, ideas and goals is dopamine.

Dopamine

Dopamine is a type of neurotransmitter but is often referred to as the chemical messenger that sends messages through our nerves. It is triggered and released when we are in a pleasurable situation or have a feeling of accomplishment. Dopamine becomes our best friend when we have ideas or goals. When an idea first comes to us and we get that rush of excitement, happiness or pleasure—that's dopamine.

Each time dopamine is released it provides us with more motivation to keep going—to achieve more—which then leads to more dopamine being released. It's easy to see why dopamine is also linked to drug usage and, in more recent years, to social media with its 'likes' and other interactions creating a vicious dopamine circle of wanting more.

A lack of dopamine can have us feeling really flat, lacking motivation, feeling like a failure, and can lead to anxiety or depression. So how do we leverage dopamine to get our motivation and drive in top gear to turn our goals into reality? Simple: we attach emotional outcomes and rewards to goals, and we chunk them down.

Emotional outcomes and rewards

There are many different ways to set strong and measurable goals. One of the most commonly referred to in the workplace is the SMART goals acronym, credited to Peter Drucker in 1954. The acronym stands for Specific, Measurable, Achievable, Realistic and Time-based. The concept assists in creating goals that are extremely clear, provide direction and leave no doubt about whether they have been achieved or not.

There are many variations of SMART, with the definition of the acronym altering slightly and the addition of ER on the end making it SMARTER goals. The ER also has variations of definitions across different industries, with NLP researchers saying that ER stands for Emotion and Reward.

I've always been a big fan of SMART goals as they give substance to ideas or dreams. The ER as Emotion and Reward is where we bring the subconscious mind into what was previously a goal deriving mostly from the conscious mind.

We know that everything we do is based on an emotional outcome, so we bring this emotional outcome into the goal to remind us of what we stand to gain in achieving the goal and what we stand to lose by not achieving it. As soon as we acknowledge and own those two potential emotional outcomes, we have linked our subconscious mind to the goal and created our 'why' and purpose.

Let's say I have the following goal:

'My husband and I will take our kids to Disney World in Orlando, Florida, for 2 weeks in July 2022.'

Applying the SMART concept, this is specific, measurable, achievable, realistic and time-based. I have a strong goal that I have all the best intentions of delivering on. If I don't deliver, I'll be disappointed, and I'll probably try it again for the following year.

Now I ask myself the question, 'Why?' Why is this goal important to me? Why do I want this to happen? How will I feel if I deliver this goal?

The answer to my 'why' is 'so that my children can experience the feeling of Disney World while they are still young': for them to have that amazing experience of walking through the gates and seeing the Cinderella castle while they are young enough to appreciate it; to create memories and to travel overseas together as a family, broadening our horizons. I will feel like my husband and I have delivered a childhood dream to our kids that I also had as a child. I know it will make them so happy and in turn will make me so happy as their mum.

Thinking about this creates the emotional connection between my goal, my subconscious mind and my emotional driver.

Now, if we get to July 2022 and I haven't achieved this goal, I'm really going to struggle. It isn't going to feel good. I am very aware of the emotional outcome that I and my family will feel at that point and if it doesn't happen, it's because I didn't meet my goal.

Attaching an emotional outcome to my goal has now lifted it to a much higher level, which also lifts my determination and motivation to achieve it.

Work goals don't tend to have the same level of emotional attachment, but there still always needs to be a 'what's in it for me?' for each team member. We need to understand and emotionally connect to the goal. We have to want to achieve it and to do this, there must be an emotional driver and outcome.

How would you feel if you achieved your goal? Why would you want to feel like that? What would the benefit be for you?

Neuroscience and psychology research discuss the potential benefits of rewards when it comes to motivation and achievement of goals. The impact of the reward on our motivation is influenced by the complexity of the learning and goal; however, there is enough research to show that 'dangling the carrot' still has a positive impact on many of us. Equally, celebration is a key part of our culture and humanity. It provides time to stop, appreciate, reflect and rejoice. Adding a reward or some form of celebration to our goals adds an extra element of emotional connection and an opportunity to increase our motivation and what we stand to achieve.

I would add to my Disney World goal the reward of staying in a Disney Resort as an overall goal, and buying new clothes before we leave or enjoying a family dinner at our favourite American restaurant the weekend before we fly out as steps within my goal. This provides that extra 'dangling carrot' and adds to the excitement. As a family, we can celebrate our achievement of getting ourselves in the ultimate mindset to fly out and live our goal.

Never underestimate the impact of reward and celebrations in the workplace either. I've seen many companies with stretch goals, especially around the end of the financial year, that move straight into the next year without really taking the time to stop, appreciate, reflect and rejoice at what has been achieved. It doesn't have to be a monetary or high-class event; it does need to connect emotionally with the team members, showing thanks and recognition, and celebrating what has been achieved.

Once we have a SMARTER goal in place, along with a strong emotional outcome and reward, it's time to get started. But where do we start? It's at this point that it can get quite overwhelming. That gap between the current state and future state can be daunting, with so much to do and so little time. Now it's time to 'chunk it down' and leverage our friend dopamine to help us get through!

Chunk it down

Chunking down our goals allows multiple opportunities to trigger dopamine and ease the overwhelm. The fitness industry does this extremely well!

> Let's say I wanted to lose 10 kilograms and 6 centimetres in six months. I meet up with my personal trainer or my health nutritionist and we set my goal. We work together each week on my plan, taking measurements, doing weigh-ins, and looking at my eating and exercise habits.
>
> Each week at weigh-in I can see progress and dopamine releases in my brain giving me more motivation to keep going, knowing I am getting closer to my goal. Even if I only lost 1 kilogram and no centimetres in my first week, I can see progress and I know it's getting me closer to the end goal. Each time progress happens, my dopamine triggers my motivation and I keep going. If I don't see that progress each week and dopamine isn't triggered, my motivation levels start to get impacted.
>
> Let's imagine that I met with my personal trainer or health nutritionist and we set my six-month goal but I didn't see them, speak to them, step on the scales or take any measurements again until the six-month mark. The goal would be really hard to achieve. I would be putting in work hoping that it kept me on track. When I fronted up for the final weigh-in at the end of the six months, if my motivation kept me going that long, it would be a nervous moment to see what I had achieved.

Chunking it down is about taking our goal and breaking it down into subgoals and actions knowing that each subgoal and action provides a chance for a dopamine release. It also takes a goal that can be quite large and time consuming and breaks it down into bite-sized pieces that our mind can process and focus on.

If we have a goal that will take 90 hours to achieve and we struggle to imagine being able to commit to, it will sound much more achievable if we view it as one hour per day for six months. Likewise, losing 10 kilos sounds like a big goal, while 1.7 kilos a month seems okay. It's still the same goal, yet our mindset is completely changed simply because of our approach.

In the workplace, we are never short of ideas and ways to do things better. Some of these ideas turn into goals or projects. Some turn into performance measures or development goals for the year. This is when it is so important to chunk down the goals to bite-sized pieces—rather than the 'set and forget' that can happen, leaving us wondering why we haven't achieved our goals and why we have been talking about the same ideas or goals for years.

There are three key steps to chunking it down:

1. Identify the three key milestones within the goal.

2. Create three actions under each subgoal.

3. Align time frames.

Figure 6 (below and overleaf) sets out a SMARTER goals worksheet, using the chunking it down method, for my goal of taking my family to Disney World.

All goals are *SMARTER* goals	Time frame	
	@ time takes	Start by
Main goal: **Take my family on a trip to Disney World in Orlando in July 2022 for 2 weeks. It will be a very proud moment for me as a mum to see my kids experience Disney and will also fulfil a dream of mine. As a reward, we will stay onsite at one of the Disney resorts.**		
1 **Subgoal:** Research the trip to understand options, best time to travel, pricing and 'bucket list' items by 14 July 2021. This will provide certainty on how realistic the time frame is and get us excited for the trip. Reward: having lunch at Varsity Bar to go over the details.	2 weeks	Start of July

Action/Activity		
1 Research TripAdvisor (read at least three blogs) and Disney website to get tips and understandings.	2 days	4 July
2 Contact three friends who have done the trip to get their thoughts and feedback.	1 week	8 July
3 Go to local travel agent to get brochures and chat with a sales member.	1 day	10 July
2 **Subgoal:** Set up a budget and savings plan by 31 July in order to have the required money for the trip by 31 January 2022. This will give me certainty that it's happening and comfort as the savings progress. Reward: matching shirts to wear at Disney World.	6 months	22 July
Action/Activity		
1 Review current family finance budget.	2 days	22 July
2 Set up a new sub bank account and automatic transfers specifically for the holiday savings.	1 day	26 July
3 Follow savings plan to meet the amount required for the holiday.	6 months	29 July
3 **Subgoal:** Book the holiday, including flights, accommodation, visas and all required Disney passes by 9 February 2022. This feeling will be absolute excitement and success! Reward: dinner at The Old Faithful to eat American and celebrate.	1 week	1 Feb
Action/Activity		
1 Apply for visas, check passports.	1 day	3 Feb
2 Book all flights and accommodation.	1 day	6 Feb
3 Book Disney passes.	1 day	8 Feb

Figure 6: SMARTER goals worksheet

Let's consider in detail each of the three steps for chunking it down, using figure 6 as an example.

1. Identify the three key milestones within the goal

Each goal that we set has major milestones. Identifying three key milestones is a great place to break it down. Most goal milestones can be aligned to research, creation and implementation.

For my Disney World goal, the key milestones might be to research the trip, set up the budget and savings plan, and book the flights, accommodation and expenses. Each one of these subgoals becomes a SMARTER goal.

So now I have my main SMARTER goal and I have three SMARTER subgoals, providing three decent opportunities for dopamine hits.

2. Create three actions under each subgoal

Let's chunk it down even further. Under each of the three subgoals, I create three actions that are required to achieve that subgoal.

My first Disney World subgoal is to research the best time to travel and the pricing and to create my 'bucket list' items by 14 July 2021. This will provide certainty on how realistic the time frame is and get us excited for the trip. Our reward is having lunch at Varsity Bar to go over the details. The three actions that sit under this subgoal are to research TripAdvisor, contact three friends and go to the local travel agent.

Now I have, within my main goal, three subgoals and actions for each subgoal. This now gives me 12 opportunities to trigger dopamine and to celebrate!

3. Align time frames

We then align a time frame to each action and subgoal based on how long they will take to deliver, working our way backwards from our end time frame. This shows clearly when we need to have started each step to keep ourselves on track.

If I reach August 2021 and my savings plan hasn't commenced, I know I'm not going to meet my plan, so I should stop right now and readjust or edit where required rather than waiting until the end.

Remember that these are our goals and it is okay to own whether we need to review and readjust them. Nothing is set in stone: be realistic and own the process as well as the end goal.

Our ideas are now no longer long-lost dreams. We are leveraging neuroscience and the release of chemicals, together with the subconscious mind, to achieve our goal, one bite at a time.

Empowering to create drive

With goals and actions in place, how do we empower others to create drive, motivation and ownership? Empowerment has got to be one of my favourite ways to trigger motivation.

> A while back, I met with a technical team where one-third of the team had extensive years of experience in their field and were known as technical experts. The other two-thirds were either new to the team or had far less experience in the more challenging technical tasks.
>
> There was a very clear divide in the team between those seen as technical experts and the rest of the team. The team felt extremely under-resourced with key dependencies in the technical experts and others craving training and development. However, there simply hadn't been time to train them. It was a catch-22. People who wanted to, and were ready to step up and learn, lacked empowerment. Those that were carrying the workload didn't have time to train others. This was sending everyone round in circles. As we dug deeper into the decisions and the working of the team, there was a reluctance to share the work based on a need for control, causing the core blockage.

This is not an unusual circumstance. I see this on a regular basis among teams across all industries. There is certainly short-term pain associated with the time it takes to provide the training, but the long-term gain comes through empowerment.

Empowerment not only creates motivation, drive and development, it utilises EI and creates a culture of engagement and performance. The key to truly empowering the whole process and person means trusting them, letting go of the control and passing it to them!

There are six steps to creating empowerment. The steps form a cycle, meaning we can't move on to the next step until the current one is ticked off. At times we might progress through the steps only to have to return to a previous step if something goes wrong. Let's walk through the six steps.

Step 1: Be able to trust

Empowerment can only happen if there is trust. We must be able to trust that the other person has the ability to do whatever we are empowering them with. If there is no trust, we have to ask ourselves, 'What would it take for me to be able to trust them enough to pass on control?' The answer might be further training, proof or justification.

The key here is to put a measure against the trust and really challenge ourselves that we are not the only ones who can do whatever we are trusting them with and if they can show us 'xyz' then we know it's time to give them a go. We could test them out by giving them 10 tasks and then checking the results. If they get 90 per cent (or whatever percentage is appropriate) of the tasks right, we can be comfortable about empowering them.

This first step is as much about our mindset as it is about their ability. It's the first step of letting go of control and accepting that others are capable of what we do. They might not do it exactly the same way—in fact they shouldn't, they should do it in their own way—but we need to know they can achieve the desired outcome.

Once we truly have trust in them and their ability, only then can we move on to step 2.

Step 2: Delegate ownership

Now we cut the apron strings. Ownership is passed on to the new owner, completely and wholeheartedly. They now own this task; it's their baby. We are not letting them have a taste of it then taking it back. We are not asking them to do just one step. We are giving them ownership of this task for them to do as they please. This needs to be very clear to everyone. If we struggle to hand this over, we go back to step 1.

Step 3: Give decision-making power

There is a big difference between asking someone to step in for you and giving them decision-making power.

Too many times I have sat in meetings where all of the stakeholders or decision makers have been invited into a room to make a decision. One of the invitees couldn't make it and has sent someone in their place. However, this person is simply a scribe. They are there to take notes. They hold no decision-making power and therefore the meeting has been a complete waste of time because we couldn't reach an end decision. This is definitely not empowerment.

If empowerment had occurred, the person in attendance would have had the ability to make the decision required right then and there. This is the difference between simple delegation and true empowerment. If we struggle to do this, we go back to step 1.

Step 4: Lead, don't tell

The temptation is always there to give people the answer or tell them how to do something, especially if we have been doing so for quite a while. Sharing knowledge and expertise feels good and with the best intentions, we feel like we are helping others.

The problem is, people generally remember where they found an answer faster than they remember the answer itself. If the answer came from us, they would remember they got it from us more easily than they would remember the actual answer. But they wouldn't easily be able to find the answer again without coming and asking us. If they found the answer themselves, they may not remember the actual answer but they could go back to wherever they found it and get it again.

Being a great leader and empowering others requires pausing—not providing the answer, but challenging the other person to really think about: 'If you were the only person here right now and you had to make a decision, what would that decision be?' Asking this question returns the full ownership to them and gets them building their confidence and their ability.

If they still don't know, ask them to guess. The word 'guess' allows them comfort in that it doesn't have to be 100 per cent right and removes some of the pressure because it's just a guess. If that doesn't help, chunk it down and ask them, 'What considerations or factors are involved?' The five questions that we covered to smash through self-doubt in chapter 6 will also help.

The key to this step is to continue asking questions, offering support and giving leading tips but not telling them the answer. Even if leading them eventually tells them where they can go to read or find the answer, we still don't give them the actual answer. I like to remind them that I trust them and will support whatever decision they make as long as they can show me the thought process that went into their decision and it's logical.

Remember, we have already delegated ownership; this is their baby and they have the decision-making power so get them to make the decision.

Step 5: Reflect

Rarely will we absolutely nail something first go. It takes repetition, practice and experience to continually grow and develop our expertise. For this reason, reflection is an absolute necessity.

We take the opportunity to stop and review the process from beginning to end. 'What worked? What didn't work?' 'Now that we know what we know, what would we do differently?' 'What were the biggest learnings/takeaways?' 'Did we achieve the purpose and desired outcome?' 'What are the next steps?'

If everything didn't go to plan and the desired outcome was not achieved, this is not the time to revoke the empowerment and take back ownership! This is the time to learn and continue to grow.

Step 6: Learn

There is always something to learn from everything we do. Sometimes we learn what not to do next time and that's okay. We sit down together and make a list of everything we learned through the process. We, as the ones empowering, and them as the person being empowered. What role did we both play and how can we learn in order to improve on it next time?

Did we completely tick off each step? Did we trust them, delegate the ownership, hand over the decision-making power and lead—not tell—while still offering full support?

Did they believe and trust in themselves? Did they own the process 100 per cent and did they make decisions based on logical, well-thought-out processes? Identify the learnings and apply them next time.

If we really want to empower others, we must start with ourselves and our mindset. When we get this right, motivation and drive will become part of the culture, lifting engagement and results.

Driving sales through modalities

Sales is all about delivering an emotional outcome. Everything we do is for an emotional driver and outcome and it's not until we have the connection between the product or service and our emotional driver that we decide to make that purchase.

The fastest way to get this connection is by receiving the message through our default modality. In chapter 5, we learned about our default modality and identifying modalities. This takes that knowledge to the next level.

This isn't just about the physical sales process. Every form of communication—whether it is a physical sale, training or getting someone to 'buy-in' to the message we are communicating—relies on an emotional connection to achieve the desired outcome. When we can identify the modality in the person we are communicating with and achieve that emotional connection, we don't actually have to sell.

We usually deliver information to other people in the same way as we prefer to receive it. This aligns to our default modality. So, given I am a highly kinaesthetic and visual person, if I were selling you a house I would show you pictures, but ultimately I would want to show you the property, walk you through and let you experience it.

The same goes for if I were training you. I would show you once or twice and then let you have a go. The problem with this is that if I were trying to sell a house to someone who is a highly digital person, they are going to want to know all of the details—the research—before they see the property. What's the area like? What are the included or nearest facilities? Average price of other properties in the market? I would be wasting both of our time showing them the property without giving them the chance to research it first as there are too many unanswered questions in their mind.

Trying to sell, train or communicate to others by taking the same approach or following the same process each time is certainly not the fastest or most effective way to operate.

First, we identify their default modality through conversation and observation. Ask them about other purchases they have made in the past and were they happy with the process. How did they decide that it was the right purchase for them? What made the process so smooth? Asking simple questions and really listening to the modalities that are described, or were used, will help us to identify what their modality is.

It's also good to ask them how they prefer to receive information from us. Would you like to see the property first, receive pictures, receive full details and a brochure? What is your preferred method of communication? Would you like me to send you emails, give you a call or catch up face-to-face? We make so many assumptions when interacting with other people when the simplest of questions can completely change the interaction and the outcome. Ask the questions and really listen to the answers.

There are some fantastic salespeople who create this connection instantly; others cover all bases by ensuring there is something for all types of modalities upfront. We notice this a lot with great presenters and trainers. There should be an element of their presentation to suit each modality: pictures, statistics, interaction and of course someone talking who they can listen to.

Our modalities are the shortcut straight through to our emotional driver and our motivation to make decisions. The faster we can identify other people's modalities and adapt our delivery, the faster we will trigger motivation and our emotional decision driver.

Managing 'busy' and leveraging peak performance

Building our motivation and drive can become a bit exhausting or overwhelming regardless of how many skills we have. Our adrenaline is pumping, and it doesn't seem like there are enough hours in the day to do everything that we want to do. The 'busy' word starts to creep in, inviting stress along with it. I heard someone describe their 'busy' last week as an intersection where the traffic lights aren't working and there are no traffic police directing the traffic. There is so much going on but really nothing is moving or progressing.

We may have heard the saying 'work smarter, not harder'. This is where we really dissect that statement to understand whether it's possible to work smarter and, if so, how. Let's talk about three of my favourite ways to leverage the functions of our brain.

Focus

A study conducted by the University of California, Irvine suggests that it takes on average 23 minutes and 15 seconds to refocus following an interruption. Let's just think about that for a moment … 23 minutes and 15 seconds. If you are lucky enough to only have maybe three interruptions in one day, that's over an hour of time every day that is used to refocus.

If you work in an environment where the phone is ringing, emails are coming in, people are asking questions or talking to you and meetings are going on, interruptions could be a given and we might find the number of interruptions in a day is much higher.

Eliminating these interruptions completely is generally not realistic. However, reducing the number of interruptions by even one credits us 23 minutes and 15 seconds back in our day, according to the study.

When I really thought about this and started to question the concept, I thought that surely some interruptions take only minutes or even seconds to refocus rather than 23 minutes and 15 seconds. There are two key factors playing into this: the complexity of the interruption and the timing. How complex was the task that we were working on before we were interrupted and how long were we interrupted for?

If it was a highly complex task and we were interrupted for long enough that our mind had to start to focus on something else, for example a phone call or a question that requires thought or knowledge, then yes, it is likely to take us 23 minutes and 15 seconds on average to regain that focus.

If it was a quick question asking if we'd like a cup of coffee, chances are the impact will be very little. If the interruption relates to what we are working on, it can actually work in our favour, so those interruptions can be welcomed!

I can certainly recall days when I have spent the majority of the day in my email inbox or on the phone. At the end of the day, I feel like I've got nothing done, yet I know I've been working hard all day. My mind has been pulled from one thing to the next and touched so many different pieces of work but really not progressed with anything.

It's very normal for us to feel like we need to instantly respond when something happens. Yes, this provides great service to the people requesting something; however, it is to the detriment of whatever it was that we were working on.

This is exactly the type of thing I'm referring to when I say work smarter, not harder. If we could limit some of those interruptions, allowing our mind more time to focus on the one task, we would achieve so much more.

How many interruptions do you have each day? How could you reduce or mitigate some of those interruptions?

There are times when we are away from our desk, perhaps in a meeting or going to the toilet or having lunch, making us unavailable to answer a phone call or an email. It's highly likely that it won't be the end of the world if we don't respond that exact instant. Can we shut down our email inbox for half an hour while working on a complex task? Could we ask someone else to cover our phone calls for an hour while we focus and then we can return them the favour? Interruption-free time will instantly provide 'time credit' back in our days. The time wasted for our mind to refocus becomes time that we can use to achieve outcomes instead.

Cycle

Tony Schwartz highlights some of the extensive research that sleep researcher Nathaniel Kleitman first discovered more than 50 years ago in relation to our ultradian rhythm. Our ultradian rhythm is a 90–120-minute cycle that is present both while we are asleep and while we are awake. These ultradian rhythms make up the 24-hour circadian cycle that our brain goes through every day. The 90–120-minute cycles have been found to work for many other researchers and industries over the years including Anders Ericsson and his study on prodigious violinists.

The 90–120-minute cycle is our brain hitting peak and low performance as we go through each cycle. We say 90–120 minutes as it varies from person to person. Some people's focus lasts closer to 90 minutes before requiring a break to maintain high performance whereas that of others can go for up to 120 minutes.

As we commence each cycle our performance is generally low and starts to build to peak performance as we head into the middle of the 90–120-minute cycle. It then starts to drop again towards the end, very much like a bell curve for each rhythm. After each rhythm, our brain needs some downtime—a chance to reset! Studies tell us that 20 minutes is the optimal amount of time for the brain to reset ready to head into another ultradian rhythm.

Of course, we know that we can keep working and push ourselves through hours upon hours of work without a break. What we need to accept is that our brain is not performing at its peak when we are doing this. This raises the question of how effective we really are when we work for five hours straight without a break compared to two cycles of 120 minutes with a break in the middle. It's common knowledge that driving for five hours without a break becomes extremely dangerous for our ability to focus and respond, and this is also relevant anytime we are using our mind. The first response for many of us is that we don't have the time in our day to take a 20-minute break every two hours!

While 20 minutes is the optimum, any type of break is better than none, as long as our brain isn't actively having to think or process anything. A trip to the kitchen for a cup of tea or a toilet break is better than no break. If I were a betting woman, I would put all my money on the quality and peak performance in a day being much higher when achieved by aligning to our ultradian rhythm and taking those 20-minute breaks rather than working straight through with no break.

Let's take it a step deeper! The level of our peak performance in each one of our ultradian rhythms throughout the day can differ. Some of us prefer mornings and therefore our first few ultradian rhythms of the day are our strongest, whereas others are more late afternoon/night-time people. Some of us peak around 10 am, then slump around midday only to peak again around 3 pm. Working out our strongest time of day and most powerful ultradian rhythm adds another layer to leveraging our peak performance.

Grab a piece of paper and note down the time you start work each day on average. Map out your day based on 90–120-minute blocks with 20-minute breaks in between. Test this out for a few days, taking note of which rhythms give you the most energy and the highest focus. These are the rhythms that we want to align the most complex tasks to. We tend to start the day checking our emails. However, if our first rhythm is our strongest, it could be wasted spent on low-complexity tasks.

If we leverage the interruption-free time that we earned from focusing, we now have a day where we are claiming back on average 23 minutes and 15 seconds for every interruption avoided and we are leveraging the peak performance of our mind with our ultradian rhythms in our most effective rhythm of the day.

How much time and performance have you credited back so far?

Let's take it one step further.

Batch

Before we head into this third way of leveraging the functions of our brain, I would only ever recommend using this step in extremely high workload periods for a short amount of time. Our brain needs stimulation and change in order to grow and develop. Without this, it is on autopilot, boredom can kick in and we can even limit the growth of new neuron pathways.

We are now very aware that we can achieve more in a set period of time if our brain isn't interrupted. It can go into autopilot and race through a list of similar items. For this reason, batching the same style of tasks together achieves higher output.

Factories and production plants are a clear example of this. With each station repeating the same step, efficiency and speed are created.

I spent a good part of my corporate career in the insurance industry. The insurance industry is part of financial services and therefore is impacted by the end of the financial year. The workload during the last month of the financial year can be triple the size of other months. This means there are very few workplaces that are staffed appropriately for this extreme peak period month each year.

The pressure is intense and the impact on the teams is huge. Training or learning is not something that was a focus during this time. Getting through the mountain of work in the set time frame was the number one priority. Batching is something that I regularly implemented for that one month to get us all through as smoothly and as sanely as possible without pulling out too much of our hair.

It's a simple concept. We can batch in two different ways: by task or by people. Batching by task is about us looking at all of the individual tasks and processes that we do and batching the same tasks together. For example, if a process that we do regularly has four steps to it, instead of doing step 1, then step 2, then step 3, then step 4, then repeating it for the next item, we do step 1 for all items, then we do step 2 for all of them, then step 3 and finally step 4. It limits the times that our brain is required to switch what it is doing and focusing on, allowing us to achieve more in a small amount of time. The downside is that we lose the big picture of concentrating on one item from beginning to end. It is also quite robot-like and doesn't engage our brain a lot. But it can be beneficial to batch things we don't enjoy doing.

When I first started my business, before I outsourced anything and it was only me working for the business, the bookkeeping side was not something I enjoyed. Doing my receipts each day was annoying and I tried to avoid it. It really was the downside to each day, so instead I decided Friday afternoon I would finish off my week by doing all of my receipts at once then head into the weekend. It removed the task that I disliked from impacting me every work day and batched it together, so it didn't take me as long to do. It was a win–win!

The second way we can batch is by people. This is where we decide that each person will do a specific step in the process, generally the one they are the best at. Our most experienced staff worked on the most complex tasks and our newest staff or staff with the lowest authority limit worked on the tasks that they had authority to do without referral or checking.

This created less checking, double handling, training and questions. It maximised our time and resources. Sadly, I see too many companies that do this consistently throughout the year rather than only in extreme peak periods. Having this approach means that no-one is being challenged, learning or growing. It's a sure way to create a big divide between experienced and less experienced staff and creates a long-term key dependency and lack of succession planning.

* * *

Let's bring these three ways to leverage the peak performance of our minds together. Focus with blocks of time minimising interruptions. Do this in 90–120-minute ultradian rhythm cycles, allocating the most complex tasks to our peak performance times of day. Batch when work really hits the extreme peak periods. This is how we work smarter not harder and start gaining good chunks of time in our day while performing at our absolute best!

Mindset over burnout

A 2018 study by Professor Michael Leiter reports that burnout can impact anywhere from 5 to 7 per cent of the Australian workforce. In addition, in 2015 Heads Up reported that one in five Australians (21%) had taken time off work in the previous 12 months because they felt stressed, anxious, depressed or mentally unhealthy. They also noted that 92 per cent of serious mental health concerns are attributed to workplace stressors.

Burnout is becoming a common term in workplaces across the world. While working smarter, not harder, will help to relieve some of this burnout, our mindset also requires work to help us get through and avoid the burnout.

While the work we have done throughout this book and the ongoing development of our EI will help us to own, face, feel, ask and drive our mindset, let's discuss four key steps to refer to in these extreme times.

Step 1: Purpose

Ask the question 'why?' Why are we doing this particular thing? What is the purpose in saying what we are about to say, walking into this meeting, writing this email...getting out of bed? Everything we do requires a purpose. The purpose should be understood and stay front of mind. This is what should be driving us and providing clarity in our mindset.

Step 2: Emotional win

What is the emotional driver and what is the emotional win? How will we feel when we achieve our purpose? Do we want to feel like that? How do we want to feel while it is happening? What triggers do we know that will create that emotional reaction during the process? How can we continue to own and face those emotions, taking control each step of the way? Owning and being very clear on our emotional win provides further purpose for what we are doing and helps to ease any overwhelm when the gain is very clear.

Step 3: Sleep

Never underestimate the need for sleep! We don't sleep just for fun—our body and our mind physically require sleep in order to function. We know through research that the recommended sleep for an adult is 7 to 9 hours every night. In order to sleep we need time to unwind our mind—sleep results when our mind stops racing and actively thinking.

As a parent, it makes me laugh how at times when my kids were young we would be playing or eating or having fun then I would look at the time and say okay bed time, expecting my kids to go straight to bed and to sleep. Their minds are the same as ours and require time to unwind and prepare for sleep. Here I was wondering, why aren't they going to sleep? Adults are the same: not only do we need sleep, but our minds require time to unwind before going to sleep.

Long hours at work and having minimal sleep is not healthy for us, nor is it healthy for the decisions and work we are doing due to lack of effective sleep. Studies by the CDC (Centers for Disease Control and Prevention) on 'drowsy driving' have shown that cognitive impairment can have the same impact as being legally drunk.

Cognitive impairment can be caused by at least 18 hours without sleep or only getting four to five hours of sleep for around four to five days. It's a scary thought that some of us, doing long hours at work with minimal sleep, could be making some very big and high-risk decisions in an equivalent state of being legally drunk! I know we would never make those decisions while drunk, or arrive at work legally drunk, so why would we do it as a result of cognitive impairment due to lack of sleep?

There are so many fantastic tools available to help us get a good night's sleep. From sleep and meditation applications through to sleep schools, find whatever works for you so that you can switch off your mind and get a great night's sleep.

I have sleep music playing each night when my husband and I go to bed. In the lead-up to this, we usually have either café jazz or relaxation music playing in the background before we go to bed. I like to sink and push my body into the bed, which makes me aware of any muscles that I have tensed or haven't yet relaxed. When this doesn't get the desired result, I turn to breathing exercises.

Step 4: Breathing

We know that it is ultimately our mind that keeps us from going to sleep. Changing the speed and depth of our breath slows down our heart rate and lowers our blood pressure. Creating relaxation across all of the organs and muscles in our body helps us to go to sleep and get the rest that our mind needs to be able to function.

There are many different breathing techniques used around the world—you can find them on the internet. Most of them work off the method of becoming aware of our breathing, our body, our muscles and what our mind is doing. The order in which they are done and the count for each step is what differs.

The breathing technique I regularly use on those nights when my mind will not stop turning is the Navy Seal Box Technique, also known as the 4×4 method. The technique is based on breathing in to the count of four, holding your breath for the count of four, breathing out to the count of four and holding for the count of four. Repeat this until you fall asleep.

I love this method as it requires my mind to count—in a similar way to counting sheep—which stops it from thinking of anything else. It slows down my breathing and helps to slow down my heart rate and blood pressure, which also relaxes all of my muscles. The oxygen cycle in my body is full and complete given I am completely emptying my lungs and refilling them each time. Meditation uses a similar process, with only the count being different. It usually has only three counts: breathing in to the count of four, holding for the count of seven and breathing out to the count of eight. There are many different breathing exercises using different counts. Find the one that works for you to achieve the desired outcome.

Never underestimate the impact of breathing. It's what keeps us alive and is the ultimate way to control our body and our mind.

When we think motivation and drive, energy and 'busy' can come to mind. Really achieving results and our desired outcome requires us to be in control rather than overwhelmed or burned out.

Leveraging the way that our mind works, our emotional drivers, the feeling of empowerment, the chemicals that are produced, the impacts of sleep and oxygen: this is how we truly create drive, turning those endless ideas into reality.

The importance of reflection

Our hippocampus is a part of our brain and is responsible for our learning and memory. Review and reflection help us to activate the hippocampus, learn faster and create memories by asking:

- What was the outcome?

- Was that the original purpose?

- What worked well?

- What didn't work so well?

- What have I learned?

- What would I do differently?

Reflection allows us the opportunity to constantly learn from every task and situation every day. Being able to pause and reflect creates self-awareness and situational awareness. EI is a constantly moving skill. Given every person and situation is different, the chance of exactly the same outcome is quite slim.

I've worked with many companies that have brilliant ideas which are lost at the project and implementation stage. The end result has veered far from the original purpose. Unfortunately, this is repeated again and again through many projects and ideas simply because the time wasn't taken to pause and reflect.

We can struggle when things don't go to plan and the desire to move on quickly and not speak about what happened becomes a natural response. Or we talk only of the positive outcomes, ignoring the elephant in the room, trying to convince ourselves that it was time and money well spent.

When there is no reflection, our ability to learn has been overlooked. Our memory recalls what we did and how we did it. The actual outcome, performance and learnings are buried, meaning when we tap into our memory, we repeat the same mistakes again.

How often we reflect comes down to personal preference. Some people like to reflect on a daily basis, some weekly—others extend the time frame even longer. In the workplace, reflection at the end of any implementation should be a given.

I like to reflect following interaction with people. The interaction will determine the extent of the reflection. After a brief interaction, I reflect simply by asking whether the outcome aligned to the purpose and what I would do differently next time. In a workshop or program, my reflection is a lot more structured and defined.

How often do you ask yourself the six questions above? How often do you reflect and continue to develop from each and every situation?

Building our EI requires ongoing reflection and self-awareness. I teach EI, and yet there are times when even I wonder how emotionally intelligent my reaction was to something. We're all human!

It's the drive within us to be motivated, to create and achieve goals while we are reflecting that will continue to build our EI.

Drive it

- Visualising our goals embeds the memories into our mind, making our mind feel like it is missing something and therefore wanting it even more.

- Creating motivation and drive is about understanding why achieving the emotional outcome is so important in the first place.

- Dopamine is a chemical messenger that provides us with motivation every time it is triggered.

- 'Chunking' our goals down to bite-sized pieces helps to trigger dopamine.

- Empowerment starts with us and our ability to trust others.

- The six key steps to empowerment are trust; delegate ownership; give decision-making power; lead, don't tell; reflect; and learn.

- Our modalities are the shortcut straight through to our emotional driver and our motivation to make decisions. The faster we can identify other people's modalities and adapt our delivery, the faster we will trigger motivation and our emotional decision driver.

- To work smarter and reach our highest potential, we must understand how the human mind functions, leverage the peak performance period and decrease the time wasted to refocus.

- We avoid burnout by gaining control of our mindset, including our purpose, emotional wins and two of our core human functions: sleeping and breathing.

- Reflection is the most effective tool for all learnings. Without reflection, our mind will default to the way it's done things in the past, resulting in the same errors occurring.

Part III

The future of EI in the workplace

While the concepts of EI date all the way back to 1990, with Peter Salovey and John Mayer, we are noticing the focus on and importance of EI in the workplace becoming a higher priority.

Over the past few years, EI has begun appearing in more 'Top 10 Future Skills to Have' lists and since the COVID-19 pandemic in 2020, it can be found in most 'Must Have' skills. The pandemic created a spotlight on the importance of people and mindsets in every workplace. While the impact on the economy was substantial, the impact on people and their mindsets became a major focus for workplaces, extending past physical health and into mental health.

Regardless of what the future brings, where people are involved the level of EI will always influence the outcome.

Chapter 10

The importance of EI in an AI world

Technology truly is amazing. The progress that technology continues to make and the rapid progress we are seeing in AI and robotics is exciting to say the least. I am often asked what is more important, EI or AI, and my response is the same as when I'm asked to choose between EI and IQ: life isn't about one or the other, it is about how they come together.

Neuroscientists and psychologists still can't explain why or how our brain does everything that it does. For this reason, I find it hard to believe that robots or AI will ever be able to do everything that the human mind can do. Not forgetting that it is human brains that design technology, AI and robots.

Programming is a result of the human brain, with most of it built around decision trees. The work that our conscious mind does, along with highly structured processes, opens the opportunity to automate. The subconscious and emotional mind is a little harder to program but isn't a complete blocker. We are seeing EI—which is programmed by humans—become part of the programming in robotics.

We know emotions drive everything we do, so it is very much a given that any form of technology or innovation that involves humans has an element of EI built in. Unfortunately, EI hasn't found its obvious role in every project process as yet. Having an EI specialist involved in each project ensures that the human element is incorporated, and that the ultimate emotional driver is considered and factored into the build.

There is always an opportunity to continue to develop EI within every person, every process and every project. The higher their levels of EI, the more emotionally intelligent the result will be. Before any project gets to the last step, we should be asking, 'How will this make people feel?' 'Is that how we want them to feel?'

These seem like simple questions; however, we know that every person thinks and feels differently. While we work towards the majority approach, there will always be the minority who don't fit into the technology solution. For those instances where the situation isn't quite so straight forward and when technology can't help, we default back to human assistance.

Have you ever spent hours trying to work something out and eventually called helpdesk for assistance, only for them to tell you that you'll find the answer in the (electronic) self-help guide?

Once we choose to engage with humans over technology, we want a human response—not to be directed back to technology. We want them to understand us and to deliver the outcome we are looking for—that is, we want them to be emotionally intelligent!

Focusing on technology and AI is absolutely an advantage, if not a necessity, for workplaces to continue to grow and develop. EI is also part of this focus and necessity. The future is about more than just technology. Technology and innovation require an emotional driver and an EI component in order to connect with humans.

The future is about the marriage between AI and EI.

Chapter 11

EI and job titles

There is speculation that some of the professions that students are studying at school and university will not exist by the time they have achieved their qualifications.

It is common for students to define their future, and measure their success, based on joining a specific profession or achieving a certain job title or pay packet. This becomes a part of the beliefs and values embedded in our subconscious mind as students, guiding many of the decisions that we make through life to build our self-worth, confidence and sense of achievement and purpose.

Due to technology moving at such a rapid pace, industries and jobs are changing at an incredible speed, creating not only uncertainty for students but also for working adults. We find ourselves questioning our definition of 'success' and whether we can actually achieve it if the profession that we studied or have been working in no longer exists.

The rapid development of technology not only impacts every industry and many job titles, but also our embedded beliefs and preconceptions of our purpose, and even for some, our self-worth.

Why do we ask teenagers *what* they are going to be when they leave school? We ask it when we are young and sometimes still ask it of ourselves as adults — *What* we are going to be when we grow up? — and feel like a failure if we don't achieve that 'statement job'. Although our intentions are well-meaning, this loaded question places the focus on *what* we should become. Perhaps we should shift the focus to defining *who* we would like to become instead. Job titles should never define us.

> When I was 17, I really disappointed my parents. In fact, my dad was very angry!
>
> Growing up, for as long as I can remember, I always had high aspirations for myself. My six-year-old self wanted to be on stage. It didn't matter what I was doing there. Whether it was singing, dancing or acting ... I just wanted to be on stage. The larger the crowd, the better. The only thing that held me back was talent.
>
> Heading into my early teens, I dreamed of being a flight attendant: the exotic lifestyle of flying to new destinations around the world with my pull-along overnight bag and smart uniform beckoned. But there were two problems: I was really quite scared of take-off, landing and any turbulence, and even at that age I was too tall.
>
> You see, back in those days, TV screens on aeroplanes were lowered from the ceiling of the plane into the aisles and for occupational health and safety, you had to be tall enough to reach the overhead lockers but short enough to walk the aisles while the screens were down without banging your head against them ... all while wearing heels. A dream killer!
>
> In my mid-teens I thought I'd like to become a primary school teacher. But a bit of work experience at the local school showed I didn't have the patience for hearing 'Miss Amy' that many times in a day.
>
> In my late teens, it was all about psychology and a fascination with the mind. Forensics, criminology and psychology. I dabbled in psychology studies but soon realised my high visual modality meant I couldn't switch off from what I was visualising, and I was taking everything on board as if it were my own problem — visuals and all. That wasn't good.
>
> Throughout these years, the one thing I was certain of was that I would be the first person in my family to go to university.

Then I changed my mind. You see, my logical brain is quite active and given I didn't know exactly what I wanted to do, I made the decision to not commit to uni straight from school and instead entered the workforce. It didn't make sense to commit the time and money when I didn't know what I wanted to be. My parents were extremely disappointed and angry. They had always been, and still are, the most supportive and amazing parents I could ask for but in this instance, they were certain I was making the wrong decision.

'You are throwing your life away! You are capable of so much more! This is the biggest mistake you could make!'

This became a major defining moment for me. At that moment, I decided to prove them wrong. I would show them that I could be successful without going to university straight out of school.

In fact, I created 'my belief' of what success looks like. Now, everyone's definition of success differs. At some point in our lives we create that belief, or we change that belief and it guides the decisions and choices we make and what we value in order to make that belief true.

For me, success became about climbing that corporate ladder until I was a manager and earning what I thought was a 'university qualified' equivalent salary. This salary changed as the years went by.

The definition of success was also tweaked with me constantly moving that 'success' measure higher as I reached each goal. I was constantly raising the bar! My final measure was executive level, with a pay packet to match.

How did I feel? I felt extremely successful! I felt like I had absolutely smashed my parents' doubts and fears and more importantly I'd proved them wrong. They were so proud of me and all that I had achieved using the ability that I always had.

I had the most amazing corporate career, which I am so thankful for. I worked with brilliant leaders, some of whom were technically great, though they lacked basic people and EI skills. Many asked me along the way, 'Amy, what direction are you heading in?'; 'Where do you see yourself next?'; 'What do you want to be?' My answer was always the same: 'As long as I'm challenged and I'm learning something new, I'm happy.'

I was promoted across all parts of the company and became a 'go to' person for anything EI or people-leadership related. I accepted leadership roles in areas in which I had no technical experience to be able to focus on the core leadership responsibilities of lifting teams that were capable of so much more and building their EI skills. I began facilitating and speaking at events on EI, which I absolutely loved doing.

However, while every leadership role had a large people-skills focus, it still had the technical strategic component and each department was different. Some I really enjoyed, others I couldn't find the love for.

How did I really feel? ... I still felt lost. I still felt like, what's next? Who needs me next? What department haven't I been to yet? What is my purpose? Where do I belong?

It's like I was constantly at a crossroads, waiting for someone to tell me the magic answer to my 'why'.

One month after I achieved my final measure of success of exec-level title and pay packet, I gave my notice of resignation.

You see, over these years, I had started to come back to my core fascination of the mind. Diving into the neurolinguistic programming of our minds, attending conferences and workshops, hearing speakers, gaining qualifications, being a speaker and trainer myself, and working with people each and every day as a leader, it started to become clear.

Throughout my whole career in the corporate world, my strengths and focus were always around the people — about lifting them to their full potential. Helping them to build their EI skills: how to become self-aware, how to control their emotions, how to motivate themselves and those around them to not just dream but achieve big.

> It was all about how others felt when I communicated, not about how I was feeling. People are guided by underlying emotional drivers, and understanding these drivers and the impact you have will determine the outcome. All of these drivers stem from the defining moments that create our beliefs and values.
>
> It was time. I had found my 'why' and it was time for me to listen to myself and act on the advice I was sharing with so many others.

Once we find what it is we love doing, it's all about increasing how often we do it. Success is being happy—it really is that simple. Find what makes you happy and incorporate as much of it into your life as you possibly can.

I never had a dream or aspiration to run my own business. I know for some people this is the ultimate goal, but I was always happy to be an employee. However, I knew that the only way to do what I loved and spread the social impact of breaking through the misconception of EI was to believe in the one (and only) thing I have total control over in life: *me*!

That 17-year-old Amy had created a belief off the back of proving her parents wrong. It was all about success being measured by a job title and a pay packet. It took me more than 20 years to realise that success is not about a job title or a pay packet. Success is about understanding and finding our 'why'. Our 'why' is not one specific thing or job title. It is not a *what*. It is *who* we are.

When I look back, that younger me had all the answers to finding her 'why' at her fingertips. The love of the stage is very much reflected in my speaking and service offerings. The primary teacher in there was desperate to teach and share knowledge, though the audience is older and aligned to the workplace. The forensic, criminal psychologist was fascinated with the strength of the mind and how to be amazing rather than the alternative. The flight attendant ... well, my family are all travel junkies and we spend all of our money on holidays.

Before there were any pressures about *what* I would become—before the judgement of others and more importantly the judgement and pressures from myself—my 'why' was right there in front of me.

It's easy to think, *if only I had realised this back when I was 17*, but the truth of the matter is, I wasn't ready for it. The path I took is what prepared me for where I am today. My 19 years in the corporate world working with people with so many different personalities day in and day out, and the different communication methods and levels of EI are worth more to me than obtaining qualifications first.

The business acumen I developed working in so many different departments across high-profile corporations helps me to run my own successful business today. I needed to take this path to find my way to where I am right now. Who I am today helps me to help those around me—both now and into the future.

What's guiding your choices? What's your measure of success? Have you found your 'why'?

Becoming emotionally intelligent

Reading a book, attending an EI workshop or doing an EI program doesn't make us emotionally intelligent. Becoming emotionally intelligent is about learning the skills and tools and then practising, practising, practising.

Review and reflection become a part of our daily mindset and the desire to grow, develop and constantly improve who we are is what creates the ongoing development of our EI. It's not *what* we know or *what* we can do. It's *how* and *why* we do it!

Index